AURORA

MW01484215

AURORA

An Alabama school teacher in Germany struggles
to keep her children during WWII after she
discovers her husband is a German spy

KF RITTER

Copyright © 2006 by KF Ritter.

Library of Congress Control Number:		2005901735
ISBN 10:	Hardcover	1-4134-8614-2
	Softcover	1-4134-8613-4
ISBN 13:	Hardcover	978-1-4134-8614-8
	Softcover	978-1-4134-8613-1

All rights reserved. No part of this book may be reproduced or transmitted in any form or by any means, electronic or mechanical, including photocopying, recording, or by any information storage and retrieval system, without permission in writing from the copyright owner.

This book was printed in the United States of America.

To order additional copies of this book, contact:
Xlibris Corporation
1-888-795-4274
www.Xlibris.com
Orders@Xlibris.com
25990

CONTENTS

Introduction 9

Background 11
Education 18
New York 20
Germany 24
Ritter Ring 41
Hamburg 45
Vati 54
War 59
Summers 67
Friends 79
Way of Life 90
Trapped 98
School and Bombs 116
Strafing 124
Operation Gomorrah 129
Gross-Flottbek 146
The Last Shot 163
Postwar Germany 169
Scotland Yard 184
Statue of Liberty 192

Epilogue 197
Sources 209

DEDICATION

The accounts on the following pages are recorded with deepest respect, gratitude, and love to commemorate our mother's long life of sacrifice and unselfishness.

INTRODUCTION

My admiration and ideals encompass simplicity, strength, sincerity, sobriety. I oppose sophistication, superficialities, speed. Aurora Evans Ritter, *Murmurings: A Record of Thoughts, Images, and Impressions Out of My Life and Memory.* (Personal Papers, circa 1985), p. 209

I HAVE COMPILED this document for my two children, Raymond Howard Wallace III and Mary Haviland Wallace Steele, and their families hoping that it might bring enrichment and appreciation to their lives and to the life of future generations. The contents support the many volatile phases in the relationship of their maternal grandparents as they encounter love, frustration, destruction, espionage, and death during World War II. Their grandmother, Mary Aurora Evans Ritter, was intensely proud of her deep Southern roots. She came from strong pioneer stock, with unwavering principles of honor, integrity, and fairness. Her childhood was steeped in the precepts of Christianity and in the importance of education and dependable work ethics. Her forefathers fought in the Revolutionary War and in the American Civil War between the States. Equally proud of his heritage was their grandfather, Nikolaus Adolf Fritz Ritter, who came from prominent aristocratic German parents whose lineage can be traced to the twelfth century. The Ritters were well educated and known for their social status and talents in the arts.

In the following narrative, I've tried to capture some of the highlights as Mother, a highly energetic and enthusiastic young lady from the Deep South, meets a romantic Prussian military officer from northern Germany and to show how World War II altered their fate.

My brother Klaus and I grew up listening to sirens and bombs and had no measure against a strife-torn childhood. To say the least, life was exciting, and boredom was not an issue because each new day was another unpredictable adventure. I thought our life as quite normal.

After we returned from Germany in mid-1946, many relatives and acquaintances urged Mother to share her wartime experiences in writing. As an English teacher, she expressed herself easily and fluently in letters, prose, and poetry. However, to force recall of personal relationships and life-threatening experiences during World War II was too emotional and disturbing for her. I've only heard repeated snippets of specific instances that I could tie to my own memory in order to recreate here the traumatic yet interesting war years of an American mother raising two children during Hitler's devastating reign. Mother loved Germany and the German people. She had an abundance of devoted friends.

The human reflex in the wake of death and destruction is a quick recalculation of priorities. Imminent danger also sparks concentration, exhilaration during calm times, and gratitude for basic survival. I can honestly say that war is the perfect theater for experiencing the extremes of all emotions. Speaking for myself, I feel that the war years have juggled my priorities in life to a satisfactory comfort zone.

Several years ago, when I applied for my top-secret clearance with the Department of the Navy, I needed Mother's assistance in reconstructing names, places, and dates from our German past. I asked so many questions, and I could see in Mother's eyes that the flashbacks were distressing to her. After about twenty minutes, she said, "That's enough now, darling. I can't anymore." Here then—with the aid of many original documents, personal and business letters, Mother's and Father's publications, thoughtful family and friends, and Klaus's support—I present to my children my best attempt at recalling historical data of my mother's heritage in Barbour County, Alabama, and her courageous struggles to survive World War II.

BACKGROUND

By now you realize that this whole thing called LIFE is just a grand adventure. A fine show. The trick is to play in it and work at it at the same time. The more kinds of people you see, and the more things you do, and the more things that happen to you, the richer you are-even if they are not pleasant things. That's LIVING. No matter what happens, good or bad, it is all enriching. Anything is better than nothing. Just being bulk in a busy world is terrifying.—

excerpt from *Letters Sage from a Mother*, compiled and edited by Nikolaus Haviland Ritter, Berlin, Germany 1993.

AURORA CAME FROM strong, Bible-preaching, pioneer stock, deeply rooted in the backwoods of Barbour County, Alabama. How could it be possible that she finds herself in the midst of a German spy ring?

My mother's maternal forefathers came from England—in Box Glove Town, Chichester, England—in 1765. After her ancestor Samuel Winslett, an impetuous young man of about sixteen years of age, shot a large fallow deer on a restricted land in Chichester, he had a choice to make: to pay a fine of 10£ or go to America for fourteen years. In April 1766, Samuel departed for America from E. Sussex at Lewis Town on the ship *Ann* with Capt. Chris Reed. He immediately liked what he saw in his new world and petitioned to be a settler. He was granted two hundred acres of land in August of 1769 from the Georgia Land Lottery in a Quaker settlement in Wrightsboro, Georgia.

In 1771, Samuel joined as a first lieutenant of the Second Company, Greene County Regiment of Militia in Georgia. He married

Mary Carson (a Quaker) in 1774 and had ten children. Samuel's eldest son, John, played and hunted with the Indians and became fluent in their language. His maternal grandfather deeded John 187.5 acres on Town Creek of the Oconee River. Because of his hunting, tracking, and language skills, he was employed in Florida as an Indian interpreter. He also appeared in Washington, D.C., in 1832 in connection with the Indian Agency Affairs before settling down in Barbour County, Alabama. John also fathered Samuel Winslett's first grandson named Carson, sometimes called John Carson, born in Jasper County, Georgia on March 4, 1799.

Ann Kendrick Walker, *Backtracking in Barbour County,* writes:

> The village had never stood still, from the day that Carson Winslett, the first white settler, built the first frame house. Green Beauchamp knew the Winsletts and left records of this family in the Chronicles. There were four brothers, Carson, Joel, Martin and Samuel. They were the sons of John Winslett and were full blooded white men . . . Beauchamp relates a peculiar accident that befell Carson. On one occasion, he was riding with Mr. Josiah Flournoy, father of General Thomas Flournoy, on the Flournoy plantation, afterwards known as the Wales Place. On the east bank of the Chattahoochee (river), Georgia troops were scouting for Indians. The two men rode nearer the bluff to get a closer view of the soldiers and were mistaken for Indians. Carson was shot in the neck, the ball entering just above the collar bone and running around the neck until it got opposite to where it entered and there lodged until it was cut out. Falling from his horse, he remounted with the aid of his companion, rode to Irwinton [now Eufaula, Alabama] where in frontier fashion, a dentist, by the name of Cleveland, removed the bullet."

John Carson Winslett's daughter, Sara Ann, married John D. Perkins in 1855. When their daughter, Nancy Frances, married John Wesley Evans in 1887, the newly weds moved to Barbour County, Alabama and had seven children: Annie Lee; Maude Elizabeth; John Oree (Jo); Foy Sollie; Fred William; Ila Belle; and Mary Aurora (nicknamed Dawn), the youngest, born on the thirtieth day of October 1898. Aurora was John Carson Winslett's great-granddaughter.

Rural Barbour County can be charming in a quaint way with its rolling hills, deep red clay fields, and abundant longleaf pines and magnolia trees. I will use excerpts from Mother's *Footsteps Courageous— the House of Perkins, Winslett, Evans* to set the stage of her birthplace: "White Oak was a railroad station, but the post office and the mailing addresses were known as White Oak Springs . . . . At its peak White Oak consisted of three well-stocked commissaries, the railroad station with a broad platform for loading and unloading cotton and community produce, a small post office, barns and lots for transient shoppers or travelers."

Aurora's uncle William Jefferson Perkins operated one of the stores and was also the postmaster. Their house was the third Barbour County home purchased or built by her grandparents. Constructed of heart of local yellow pine, hand-planed, and painted snow-white, it sat amid magnolias on a hillside, facing east and west. It was called a double-pen house with two unusual columns to the front and one to the rear, with a central hall going all the way through the middle. There were three rooms on either side with verandas joining all the rooms. It had a parlor and a "preacher room," which were off-limits except on special occasions, and a white picket fence to separate the grounds from the road. Mother describes their daily routine:

"I recall not one day in the lives of my parents that they did not awaken long before the sun came up. 'Get a move on' became my father's perpetual greeting. A glowing fire in the large open chimney in winter, a fire in the long-legged kitchen stove, fresh coffee, and the kettle on for hot water—a good breakfast started each day. Served always on a white linen cloth on our long dining table, it too was routine. Hot homemade biscuits with syrup or jams made from our own produce and an assortment of home-cured meats were routine. My father, at the head of the table, said his usual blessing. Not a word of likes or dislikes concerning foods was tolerated. No one arose haphazardly from the table. Conversation was an adult privilege—which often bored us, especially on Sundays when there was company. As Preacher Haskew's prayer trailed on and on, moving from a strong stentorian tone to a trembling whisper, we could contain our laughter no longer and began winking, punching, and kicking under the table until the glaring eyes of our parents suppressed us."

Table conversations frequently centered on accounts of family members' sufferings in wars. She remembers: "Grandfather Andrew Evans was killed in the Battle of Chickamauga in 1863, and Grandfather John D. Perkins, with frozen sinews in the midst of winter, walked from Virginia back to his Alabama home [War of 1861-65]. When his family saw him approaching, they all excitedly happy rushed out to greet him. Grandfather said, 'Do not touch me. I'm covered with lice. Bring me warm water, soap, clean clothes, and let me change in the carriage house.'" Also, she recalls how her grandmother, Sarah Ann Winslett, told them about Indian battles and how following the fight the Winslett children would collect the colorful Indian beads scattered on the battleground and sew them on their clothing.

Mother remembers her home life as firm but with love and affection. She admired and respected her mother's pioneer grit while at the same time applying her dignified character to their standard of living. She never saw her mother corseted without a high lace collar, yet when her oldest son, Jo, severed his toe while chopping wood, she was able to sew it back on until a doctor could be reached. Mother's brothers said their father was stricter on the boys than the girls, and strappings were not uncommon. About her father she writes in Footsteps Courageous: "The seven Perkins children literally worshiped their father. Of all men he was the most temperate. He abhorred alcohol in any and every form and knowingly never touched a drop. He died of dysentery. In his final hour the doctor advised whiskey as a possible medicine to strengthen his weakening body. Grandfather Perkins stoically replied, "Doc, I've lived without the stuff all of my years. If that's the answer now, I choose to go on home."" Mother's father also advised his four sons, "Do not get in trouble and expect your father to tell a lie for you. That I will never do."

The only spanking Mother ever received, so she tells, was when she repeatedly played tricks on horseback riders as they clopped along the unpaved road near their home. The trick was to tie a string to a coin purse, drop the purse on the road, and then run the string into the bushes and wait for someone to discover the purse. When the rider approached and dismounted to grab his find, she quickly yanked the string and sprinted out of sight. She had been cautioned repeatedly by her father not to tease the travelers. On one particular occasion, as she waited quietly in the bushes, the rider got off his horse and bent down to retrieve the purse just as she snatched it away. To her horror, she recognized her father. It was too late. She had been spotted. The result was unpleasant. Mother said she never tricked anyone again. Her brothers too were full of pranks. Fred, her youngest brother, confessed that he and his male siblings ran ahead of the church crowd and hid under wooden-plank catwalks. This vantage point proved to be an effective way of peeking up through the cracks between the slats as the ladies strolled across the overpass with their full skirts. In his old age, he confessed they didn't see much, but it still was worth the excitement.

Mother was fond of talking about how her oldest brother carried her piggyback three miles home from school and how her cat refused to let anyone, except Mother, near her kittens. She also had stories about their mules, Queen and Laura and their red and white canine, Taters. Besides eating sweet potatoes, Taters loved cars. Whenever he heard a car coming, he took a running start and dashed alongside the Model T until he could leap on the running board. Once on the running board, Taters firmly pressed his body against the car door and rode until the car came to a stop. If Taters didn't find his way home alone, the driver of the car would bring him back to White Oak. Taters became a well known dog in Barbour County. Sundays were formal, of course. All the children sat properly at the table, including the preacher and their old maid, Aunt Sis, who lived with them. Aunt Sis was sitting with her back to the window and the mood was sublime when the preacher looked across at her and exclaimed in the most reverent tone, "Oh, Aunt Sis, what beautiful scenery you have behind." This triggered convulsive giggling among the children until they caught the stern eyes of their parents. Nevertheless, Mother recalls her home as one totally void of meanness, harsh language, or vociferous behavior.

Mother writes:

"In our home promises were as sacred as life itself. Word of honor, faith, obedience, truth, were real qualities and they were taught as relevant in the making of man. Worthiness was won by the goals that one set for himself. Money couldn't purchase it. Marriage, the family and the children were patterned. Everything revolved around the home, divorce was frowned upon. One married for better or for worse, and happiness was hardly considered the ingredient of success. Parents knew clearly their roles and obligations and expected little more than a week of hard work illuminated by diversions on Saturday afternoons and Sundays. Meeting one's responsibilities was fulfillment."

This solid foundation proved to be the catalyst that gave Mother the strength to survive the hardships to come.

Nancy Frances Perkins Evans (Aurora's mother)

Aurora

EDUCATION

Learning always complicates life. Illiterate humble people who live close to nature and to God may know less but understand more. Then the main all education should teach one is careful discrimination and selectivity. A. E. Ritter, *Murmurings*, pp. 205, 210

AFTER LEAVING WHITE Oak's one-room schoolhouse, Mother attended Montevallo Preparatory College and then graduated from Alabama State Normal College at Troy in 1918. She was the youngest student in the graduating class, having had special permission to do double work for two years. She also had one year of English, education, art, etc., at the Alabama College for Women in Montevallo, now University of Montevallo. Mother was at school in 1916 when her mother, quite unexpectedly, died from a misdiagnosed illness. Barely nineteen years of age, she began teaching adolescent young men and ladies (many of whom were older than she) in the Laverne High School in Alabama. After five years of teaching in Alabama, she took a state examination that qualified her for a lifetime Alabama teacher's certificate.

Mother was born with boundless energy and an optimistic personality. Her active social life, rich with interesting friends and suitors, was imperative to her temperament. She never met anyone with whom she did not find some common bond. She was popular as a student and in her professional life. Mother told me that she fell madly in love with each of her boyfriends. Finally, while teaching in Alabama, she thought she was ready for marriage and accepted an engagement ring from a well established businessman in Montevallo,

Alabama. Not long after her engagement, she received an offer for a teaching position in Florida. The wanderlust was too great and she signed a contract to teach in Florida. Her fiancé followed to set a date for their wedding. However, still in her early 20s, Mother was too energized about her career and an adventurous future to settle down. She broke the engagement. Besides, her fiancé's breath always reeked of alcohol. Although Mother was raised in a teetotaler family, she enjoyed Champaign tremendously as well as an occasional party cigarette. In any case, to marry a liquor-loving man was too risky.

Five years in Alabama and one year in Florida for a salary of $60 a month were the ultimate qualifications before attending a prestigious university for a summer refresher course. Columbia University in New York City was highly recommended. Thus, with the summer vacation of 1924 and a reservation in the Martha Washington Hotel, a ladies' refuge, she arrived on Manhattan Island—little realizing that this would be her home for the next thirteen years.

NEW YORK

As I saw the future, something wonderful awaited me. A. E. Ritter,
Murmurings, p. 40

MOTHER WAS A good student with teaching experience, and
on one occasion her English instructor at Columbia University asked
her to substitute for him during his absence. Afterward, one of her
classmates, Nikolaus Adolf Fritz Ritter (Niko), slipped her a note,
introduced himself, congratulated her for an excellent job, and asked
if she would assist him in English. The teacher humorously
intercepted the note and answered yes for her. Upon returning to
her hotel room that evening, she found a dozen American Beauty
roses.

Niko's early education was in a Prussian Military Academy. He
attended the Prussian Technical School for Textiles in Sorau in the
Niederlausitz region, a manufacturing city noted for its textiles and
porcelains. (Originally located in the province of Brandenburg, Sorau
(Zary in Polish) was assigned to Poland at the Potsdam conference
in 1945) The city of Zary lies approximately 100 miles southeast of
Berlin. His first professional position was as director of a textile factory
in Silesia which is located in the triangle of Poland, Czech Republic,
and Germany. After World War I (1914-1918), the German (Weimar)
republic faltered, partially as a consequence of defaults on war
reparations and partially because German politicians betrayed their
constituents by signing the armistice and the Treaty of Versailles,
which had unreasonable terms for reconstruction. To pay their
enormous war debts, the Germans borrowed heavily and printed

more and more paper money. By 1923 inflation was out of control. In November of that year, one loaf of bread cost 140 billion Marks. Mark notes were used to fuel kitchen stoves since paper money was less valuable than firewood. Workers were given two to three thirty-minute breaks to rush to stores to purchase anything before the Mark halved in value. The money presses were printing twenty trillion Mark notes. Germany was in a state of crisis, and America was the place to be. When Niko's paternal uncle, sent him money to come to New York, he didn't hesitate and left Germany on December 19, 1923, on the SS *Bremen* and arrived at the port of New York on January 1, 1924. He was admitted to the United States on a quota visa for permanent residence. Niko was twenty-four years old.

Niko, or Vati (German for "father"), and Mother continued their courtship even as Mother moved to her new teaching job in the Catskill Mountains. Life was too exciting for her to think about marriage. However, Niko was persistent, and on May 4, 1926, they were married and moved to 527 Seventh Street in West New York, New Jersey.

Mother supported herself and Vati by substituting in the city schools and teaching English to a host of foreigners in the Berlitz School of Languages on Broadway. After receiving a contract to teach in the secondary schools of West New York, New Jersey, she opened her own private evening classes, teaching English to foreigners using the familiar Berlitz method. She opened with a minimum of twenty students, and in less than six weeks, she had more than two hundred. Vati sought jobs in his field as a textile engineer. Animosity toward Germany still remained after World War I, and several businesses posted signs over the door, "No Germans need apply." Although he was refused many positions, Mother said that during the first year of marriage, Vati had twenty-two different jobs. Despite his charm, he was not able to remain employed. Mostly, this attitude resulted from his upbringing and his mother's disposition towards the laboring classes.

My father definitely considered himself of upper-class nobility and was not keen on taking orders from individuals whom he considered of subordinate social standing. Whether his background in the Prussian military environment contributed to this or whether his quest for self-aggrandizement conflicted with the positions offered to him is unclear. But whatever the case, Mother paid all the bills and put food on the table. Vati never lost his charisma or his charm and continued showering Mother with flowers and gifts—using her money. Mother was not confrontational. She was taught that men were to be respected simply because they were masculine. He was never fired, he always walked out because of a disagreement, and he was too proud to take his final wages with him. Mother worked on and on, making money, paying bills, and taking care of their home. However, despite frustrations, she says she was happy and that she and Vati had many glamorous, adventure-filled times together.

She and my father became members of an international club—an anti-Communist club composed of escaped Russians and others fleeing Communism. Vati had a good sense of humor and was clever and appreciative of Mother's energy. Vati loved parties and glamour. One Christmas, he spent hours meticulously decorating the Christmas tree in their apartment. Each individual strand of tinsel had to be placed precisely so it would hang straight. Finally, on Christmas Eve, the tree was lit with real candles, setting the mood for a romantic evening. As the candles flickered to a nub, so did the tree. It burst into flames and took most of the apartment with it. But when you're young and in love, nothing is overly traumatic.

Mother was glamorous and coquettish with bright blue eyes and a head full of thick auburn hair. Vati was handsome and always the formal gentleman who pressed his trousers each night under the mattress. He was proud and stylishly dressed with vest; hat; cane; and, frequently, gloves. They were often mistaken for lovers rather than a married couple. Mother told of an occasion where she and Vati stayed in a hotel in New York, and the management put a copy of D. H. Lawrence's *Lady Chatterley's Lover* on their bed, hinting at their infidelity. They traveled often, and Mother took Vati to Alabama and Georgia to meet her family. In a letter, she writes, "Prior to the birth of our children, the interluding years were perhaps the most interesting of my life."

1926 Mother and Vati (right) in New York

Vati as cadet in Prussia

GERMANY

When I married a German, I became aware of folding away a certain section of my roots. A. E. Ritter, *Murmurings*, p. 74

IN SPRING 1930, VATI took Mother to Germany to visit his family. The Ritter family lived in an imposing two-story house in Verden an der Aller, a historic town with a population at that time of fifteen thousand and located about sixty miles southeast of Hamburg. Vati was born at Houptstrasse No. 111 in Rheydt am Rhine, Germany, about 180 miles southwest of Verden, close to the Netherlands' border. He was the oldest of six children. His siblings, in order, were Gertrud, Walther Felix, Wolfgang Friederich, Anna Louise (Anneliese), and Hans Walther. Anneliese, who never married, lived in the home with my grandparents. Gertrud died at age seventeen in 1917, and I have no record of what happened to Felix. We never knew him.

Generically, the Ritters' genealogy records date the family to 1192 when the then chief was granted territory for services rendered in the third crusade. The Ritter Castle in Büdingen, Hesse-Darmstadt, the ruins which were still standing in 1648, was built by a son of the Crusader about the year 1210-15. Elias Ritter and family furnished man and munitions to the Protestant cause during the Thirty-Years-War. He was exiled, and his property confiscated. He went to England and joined an expedition sent out by Lord Baltimore to Maryland in 1650 and settled in the eastern part of Anne Arundel County.

Specifically, sixteenth- and seventeenth-century genealogical records trace our family line of Ritters to the cities of Wolfhagen and

Homburg (not Hamburg) in Hessen, Germany. My grandfather (*Opa*), Nikolaus Joseph Ritter, born in Wolfhagen, was a *studiendirektor* (school director or president) of a liberal-arts college in Verden. In addition to his directorship, he taught ancient languages and fencing. He was fair, thin, just under six feet tall; had platinum blond hair and blue eyes; and sported a mustache. He was a formal gentleman, exceedingly industrious, and fair. My grandmother (Oma) was born a Hellhof, or Hellhoff. In my research, I have seen her first name spelled four different ways: Katharine/Catharina/Katharina/ Käthe. "Käthe" is usually a nickname for Katharina, but "Käthe" is the preferred name given in several documents, including her death announcement (1876-1969). Oma could be exceedingly critical and opinionated but also displayed a great deal of charm and a good sense of humor. Oma was of average height, thin, beautiful, and always stylishly dressed. I mean *always*. She had a perfect complexion, with naturally curly hair parted in the middle and pulled back into a soft bun. Mother said Oma was almost totally gray in her late thirties. Since I knew her, she rarely wore anything except dark blue or black ankle-length ensembles with up to seven petticoats, depending on the weather temperature. In hot weather, a white blouse was acceptable. Oma was too vain to put reading glasses on her nose, but she kept a lorgnette within reach. She was convinced that anyone over fifty should only wear dark colors or be classified as *Bauersleute* (peasants). Oma came from an eminent background. She was accustomed to servants, fine china, and lace and wanted to be surrounded with glitz and glamour. One of Oma's brothers, Heinrich Hellhof (1868-1914), was a well-known painter in Berlin. He was killed in World War I. His accomplishments can be found in Brun's "*Schweizerisches Kunstler*" as well as other reference materials. In 1999, Sotheby's had one of his paintings, *Portrait of a Seated Lady*, on auction for $35,000. He was primarily well-known for his portraits of famous statesmen and royalty, including Kaiser Wilhelm II's portrait painted for the German provincial court.

Opa and Mother had much in common and immediately formed a deep mutual respect for each other. They both had practical sense, and were down to earth, realistic, and not afraid of hard work. Anneliese (Annenie to Klaus and me) too fit that description. Oma and Vati, on the other hand, loved finery and recognition but were not willing to labor for it. Vati and Mother stayed in Verden for some months. Mother said these were happy times, and she met my father's brothers, Hans and Wolfgang. I'm not sure what Hans's position in life was at this time. He was single and traveled all over the world. Wolfgang was a music student and later became a director of music for a gymnasium in Hanover, Germany. The Ritters were playful, and Mother had many pleasant memories of how the family would hike across meadows and wooded lands, always ready for a picnic. Cheese, bread, fruit, pastries, juice, or wine were an integral part of social events. Frequently, they took their bicycles with them on the train. They were familiar with the many fifteenth- and sixteenth-century towns and enjoyed cycling among the romance of their quaint architecture. Their backyard and the banks of the Aller River below the Ritter home were of equal enjoyment for games, teas, or swimming. She once told of a urination contest among the Ritter men that took place in Oma and Opa's backyard to see which of the men could aim their stream highest against the wall. They were colorful, charismatic adult children who kept a stiff upper lip but had the unique gift of turning any gathering of family or friends into a merry celebration.

Below is Mother's first impression of Germany and the Ritter family as she describes it to her sister Annie Lee Fenn in Clayton, Alabama, on Norddeutscher Lloyd's *Bremen Europa* line stationery in 1930:

Dearest Annie Lee, & family!

Here we are completely across the Continent though I cannot realize that I am almost five thousand miles from all of you! I think of each one of you at home a dozen times each day & wish so much that you might also see the things that I see. The trip across the water was restful, and enjoyable. Some kind of announcement was given each evening with dancing! And what shall I say of Europe after so much has been written & said? The clothes worn here are decidedly the same as in America, but I find that the homes, the hand work, the beautiful fields & gardens are much more cared for & kept in orderly manner. Each little spot of earth is cultivated & arranged in perfect order! The part of Europe that I have thus far seen is systematically perfect. Here in Verden are many buildings hundreds of years old, & are used daily! Much love to each, Aurora.

P.S. Nikolaus's family are ever so good to me. Our room was lovely with flower wreathes, handwork, etc. & especially painted for Nikolaus and me. All of the six children in the family (4 boys & 1 girl) are well educated and from Europe's oldest and best blood. Mutter Ritter is adorable, Vater Ritter is also dear, but decidedly strict and formal! Will write more later.

When you write me, remember that I am here in the family and they will most probably wish to read your letters. After two weeks, about the 10th of June, Nikolaus and I are going on a trip throughout the most interesting section of Germany and perhaps Paris. It will then be about the end of June or the 1st of July before we return to Nikolaus' people. You can remember that in writing me. A letter from Clayton to Germany will take about a week.

Opa, Oma, Anneliese, Wolfgang, unknown, unknown, and Hans at far right.

Mother with friend aboard ship to Germany

Grandfather Ritter

After meeting her new in-laws and traveling within the European continent for the first time, Mother and Vati returned to the United States. In 1929, a friend, Dr. Edmund F. Kohl, M.D., 313 East 86th Street, New York, offered Mother a partnership in his Morningside Hospital in Manhattan at Sixty West 120 Street, one of the largest privately owned hospitals in New York at the time. She bought one half interest in the hospital and became the administrator, and Dr. Kohl was the head physician. For convenience, Mother and Vati moved to an apartment on the top floor of the hospital. The hospital was directly adjacent to a Catholic convent with side windows facing each other, loft to ground floor, across a narrow alleyway. Mother told of interesting observations of her neighbors' clandestine liaisons as nuns and priests chased each other in playful fashion in the lighted stairwell and disappeared behind closed doors. She also was a witness to unfortunate mishaps at the hospital, such as the young streetwalker with severe abdominal pain who was brought into the hospital by the police and misdiagnosed by doctors to be drunk or drugged. She died in the hospital from a burst appendix. Mother worked hard and was able to manage complicated finances and personnel problems without creating conflicts. She loved her work and was financially able to take advantage of the many stock opportunities created by the 1929 market crash. Among others, Mother bought Coca-Cola stock, property where the New Jersey Turnpike was later built, and swampland in the most southern tip of Florida—which is now Miami. She also bought a new Ford. She and Dr. Kohl were a successful team. However, my father didn't get along with Dr. Kohl, and the feeling was mutual. Mother continued to work at the hospital, but frustrations mounted.

After nearly eight years of marriage, Mother and Vati began their family. In 1933, while she was expecting her first child, her father, who was living in Macon, Georgia with her oldest brother, Joe, died suddenly. Nikolaus Haviland, Klaus for short, was born at the Medical Arts Sanatorium, Fifty-seven West Fifty-seventh Street, New York, New York; and I came along shortly afterward at the New York Polyclinic Medical School and Hospital, 3940 Forty-sixth Street, Manhattan, New York, New York. Mother said I was born in the same hospital where Rudolph Valentino died in 1926 of septicemia, and in the same room where William Sydney Porter (O. Henry) died in 1910 of cirrhosis. Klaus decided to come unexpectedly on a weekend, and the doctor had to be called from home. He was impatient and used forceps to aid in the birth. The forceps slipped and caught Klaus in the eye. His eye was literally hanging on his cheek when they brought him to Mother. Doctors immediately wanted to remove the eye to keep it from affecting the good eye. Mother refused. She said she spent over $2,000 just to save his eye—a lot of money in the 1930s. The doctors did not take responsibility for their mistakes, and suing a doctor was unheard of. The eye slowly receded, but he remains blind in one eye to this day. The impairment and many examinations made Klaus a nervous baby. When I came along, Mother shared a hospital room with a lady from Greece who gave birth to a baby girl the same day. When the nurse brought me to Mother, all bundled up, she refused to take me and insisted that the hospital had made a mistake. She said I belonged to the Greek lady since I was born with thick black hair, and her sisters had only boys. She felt certain they had accidentally mixed her baby with the Greek mother's. Klaus had a severe case of whooping cough at the same time I was born, and Mother was not able to bring me home from the hospital for several weeks. Vati was not a patient man and, like many fathers of that time, took little responsibility in the home or with his children—except to play. Vati always enjoyed playing with us. Not long after we were born, my paternal grandfather, became gravely ill with inoperable ulcers and wanted to see his only grandchildren before he died. The four of us left by an ocean liner from New York for Bremerhaven, Germany, and, from there, to Verden an der Aller.

After several months with the Ritters, Vati returned to America; and Mother, Klaus, and I were to remain in Germany until he could send money for us to come back home. Oma said she was not going to support an American and two children indefinitely and that Mother would have to find some other place to live. Of course, Mother spoke little to no German and was literally put out onto the street with two babies and no money. She took us to Bremen, a large city twelve miles northwest of Verden, where German social services took Klaus and me away from Mother because she had no home and no immediate skill to earn money. She only spoke of this incident once, and then hesitantly and fleetingly. As one might expect, it really was a shocking and humiliating experience. She told me she did other people's dirty laundry so she could earn money enough to pay for a place where we could be together.

Vati, of course, was back in New York. Below is a letter (circa early '37) he wrote to Mother, expressing his loneliness for her. He also included information regarding a contact for her to pursue on his behalf for a position in the German military. The script is difficult to read, so I copied it.

Dearest Sweetheart!

Just received your letter with the Europa and cabled you accordingly! The boat leaves in a few hours and there is not time for a long letter. Am working at the P.O.! After the first blow it's rather funny that I'm quite calm now, perhaps even a little relieved since I *did* accidentally read your last letter first. You know Sweetheart, that nothing will take you away from me. I think I love you more now than ever before if that is possible. I know what you must have been through and that feeling hasn't made things any easier for me here. How I had hoped today to receive my call to the Army! And instead I got your letter! The thing that hurts me most, though, is that the children were taken away from you indefinitely after you had finally gotten your freedom!! How did you ever find such a nice place, love? And so reasonable! You couldn't live on that same amount of Dollars here!—But I'm now only thinking of facing a final decision. If you only knew how this uncertainty drags me down. I want to go back. I want a home there with you and the children and settle down and give you all the things I have deprived you of all these years. And that's what hurts most, more than anything else. I do hope you'll find Klevermann in. He's a real gentleman and will do everything he can for me and for you. Forget the bitterness of the last weeks and try to enjoy Bremen and learn to see Germany the way it really is. I love you with all my heart and long for you and the children.

Niko

On the back of the original letter, Vati makes this note:

Ritter Marthahous (?) Osterstrasse Bremen
   All my love—don't worry. Anxiously ready to return. See
Houptmann Klevermann today. Bezirkskommander zwei near
Bahnhof cable final decision. Niko
   Try to see Frau Lindner. You'll get her address from Rebien
at the North-German Lloydt (Zahlmeister O. Lindner, S.S.
Europa.)

(Check re submitting the original with regard to Houptmann
Klevermann).

Referring to Vati's letter, I'm not sure what was meant by "taken
away from you indefinitely" and "gotten your freedom" or who took
us away from Mother. Maybe it was freedom from her elites mother-
in-law's criticisms. At any rate, this incident remains a mystery.
   Vati had no permanent work in New York and liquidated all of
Mother's investments. He sold all of her Coca-Cola stock, her property
on the New Jersey Turnpike, and all of the Miami land, as well as her
car. Mother, of course, was eager for Vati to return and find
employment. With the contacts he provided, she interceded on his
behalf to find a position for him in the German military. As Vati
instructed, she met with Hauptman (captain) Klevermann, who was
reticent to hire an applicant whom he had never met. Klevermann
was a likeable person and was astonished at Mother's persistence.
(This is not an unusual trait for Mother. She was one of the most
stubborn and determined people I've ever known. I'm sure
Klevermann never had a chance to say no.) He told Mother that it
was an absolutely unheard-of situation where an American wife
requests employment on behalf of her German husband into the
German military. Hauptman Klevermann agreed to give Vati a "try."
If he fit in, perhaps he could be made permanent. Mother was
desperate. She wrote Vati to come to Germany and that Klevermann
would give him a chance to prove himself. Vati immediately made
plans to return to Germany by an ocean liner. The day his ship was
to arrive at the dock in Bremerhaven, a port twenty-seven miles north
of Bremen on the North Sea, Mother waited for him to disembark

with the other passengers. She waited and waited and remembers straining as her eyes scanned the deck to identify Niko. She thought he had missed his voyage. Finally, she spotted him on the top deck with the first-class passengers. She was speechless. We hardly had food to eat or money to keep a roof over our heads, and Vati was coming back in luxury. He had borrowed $2,000 from Mother's brothers in Macon, Georgia, to return to Germany—first-class.

Vati's fluency in foreign languages, specifically French and English, was quickly acknowledged by the German military. Contrary to British English spoken by most Germans, he spoke "American" English with all its idioms and slang. He was assigned to the *oberkommando* of the Wehrmacht Foreign Office under Admiral Wilhelm Canaris in Hamburg. Wehrmacht was the name of the armed forces of Germany from 1935 to 1945. It replaced the old Reichswehr and was succeeded by the current Bundeswehr. Admiral Canaris was chief of the German Abwehr (1935-1944), which is the Intelligence Department of the German Armed Forces High Command. According to the Central Intelligence Agency's files, Canaris was one of the senior officials to conclude that Germany would lose the war. (Once, after the admiral had delivered a pessimistic assessment of operations on the eastern front while briefing the high command, Hitler grabbed him by the lapels and demanded to know whether he was a defeatist.) Never a member of the National Socialist (Nazi) Party, Canaris permitted some of his officers to use the Abwehr as cover for political and religious dissidents such as Pastor Dietrich Bonhoeffer.

For us, life was pretty good again. There was no war, and Mother only knew that Vati had found his niche in the Abwehr. Our apartment in Bremen was on a canal or the Weser River, Rosenkranz Thirty-three. I was too young to remember much of life in Bremen, but by hearing Mother repeat some of the memorable occasions, they seem to become real. She always said we were "cute" children and enjoyed life. She remembered that upon returning from a social evening with Vati, she tiptoed quietly into our bedroom to check on her sleeping children. She said all she could see when she entered our room were two big shiny eyes. Upon coming closer, she was surprised to find me standing at the foot of the crib with a totally blackened face. Klaus had taken her mascara and methodically covered my entire face—inch by inch. She said after the shock wore off, she went into hysterics, laughing, but that it was a painful chore for both of us to remove the mascara. Also, Klaus and I had our personal drinking mugs, and the two of us were standing over the balcony, facing the Weser, when Klaus said to me, "Let's stretch our arms out over the balcony and hold our cups out, and on the count of three, we both drop our mugs." Well, he counted to three, and of course, like an obedient sister, I dropped my mug when he said three, but Klaus didn't. It was early childhood trauma. Worse than war. I nagged and pouted for days. I felt betrayed.

Klaus was an active little kid. Once, curiosity made him stick his head between two wrought-iron balusters of our backyard balcony railing to see what was below. It was easy to push his head forward between the stanchions, but as he tried to back out, his ears got in the way, and he was stuck. He screamed uncontrollably. Mother ran outside and snapped his picture—front and center. On a more dangerous note, while Mother was doing laundry in the basement, Klaus was crawling on the floor, investigating his surroundings. When he was ready to stand up, he braced himself on the flaming, hot furnace. His skin literally fried onto the hot metal. Both hands had to be treated for third-degree burns. Luckily, no permanent damage ensued. We never had a dull day in Germany.

Vati rallied in his new position and continued to be the charming husband and proud gentleman. Whenever Mother and Vati took a stroll or went shopping, she had to carry the bags and push the carriage and hold on to us children—all at the same time. Vati would never be seen displaying pedestrian or working-class behaviors. His posture was stiff and formal as he walked alongside in a three-piece suit, hat, gloves, and cane. She said she never saw him at the dinner table without his coat and vest. I don't have a vision of ever living under the same roof with him. Mother said he was impatient and strict and would pound his fist on the table so hard it splashed the drinks when Klaus or I misbehaved at dinner. However, he had his soft spots. Mother recalled that on a blustery, snowy evening, my father came home from work with his overcoat all puffed up. Mother asked him what he had stuffed under his coat, and he pulled out a tiny nearly frozen kitten. He found the kitty hunched up in the snow on the way home and couldn't leave it to die.

Vati was prospering in his new position as head of the air-intelligence section. His primary function was to obtain information on England's Royal Air Force and the aircraft industry in America. Upon learning that his new mission had been extended to include gathering information on the U.S. Army Air Corps (which became the U.S. Army Air Force in June 20, 1941) and aviation industry of the United States, he is quoted by Ladislas Farago in *The Game of the Foxes* as saying:

I leaned back in my chair and stared for a long time at those cold lines. Their implications took my breath. All I could think or feel was that they meant for me a new and grave responsibility. For the moment I forgot my surroundings and my new work. My life in the United States, with all its ups and downs, passed in review before my eyes. It was difficult to reconcile myself to the idea of working against the country which I loved best next to my own native land.

Mother said that Vati had frequent company in our Bremen apartment. The visitors routinely consisted of two, three, or more men engaging in intense meetings that extended late into the night. She said the group sat for hours hovered around their dining table in deep concentrated discussions. Although curious, Mother saw no particular reason to mistrust or question Vati's associations. Their relationship was congenial. Honor, trust, and obey—that's the way she was raised. When she asked him why the nameplate on their Bremen apartment door had been changed from "Ritter" to "Dr. N. A. F. Renken," Vati blew it off as nothing and said it probably was the name of a previous tenant.

Among his influential co-workers in Bremen was his secretary, Irmgard von Klitzing. Irmgard was rather tall, large boned, not pretty, but young and stylish. Mother liked Irmgard and often had her for dinner. When Vati would come home from work, he frequently had a small flower in the buttonhole of his lapel. He would say Irmgard gave it to him. Irmgard came from a prominent background with lineage to one of the German kaisers; this really impressed Vati. Also, Irmgard was politically influential within the Abwehr and was a member of the Nazi Party. She had important Party connections that would boost Vati's relationships in the espionage community. Gradually, with not-so-subtle encouragement from Irmgard, Vati and Irmgard's relationship intensified and became more than platonic. At the same time, Adolf Hitler, a micromanager and an ever-strengthening force in Germany, was discouraging his officers from engaging in close personal relationships with foreigners. Vati was receiving increasing pressure from his superiors to "do something" about his American wife. Although no direct attempts were made on Mother's life, she saw signs that gave her pause and made her feel ever more uneasy in her relationship as the wife of a German officer working with the Abwehr. Though still not totally aware of his importance in the Abwehr and his intense immersion in espionage activities against England and the United States, it became clear to Mother that her husband was affiliated with clandestine activities and using code-names. In Germany, he usually stuck with code-names closely resembling his real name such as "Renken" or "Rantzau."

Vati made no secret of the fact that he had grown fond of America but was no friend to Great Britain. Although he continued to express his love for Mother, the combination of Irmgard's advances, intelligence responsibilities, and bureau pressure created insurmountable tension and stress in our family. Vati was completely torn between his political ambitions impelled by Irmgard's support and clout, and his emotional ties and affection for his wife and children. Mother made the choice to file for divorce. Vati fought back—at least for Klaus and me.

At the height of our family turmoil, Oma paid a visit to Bremen and spoke harsh words to her son upon learning of his relationship with Irmgard. She was furious with her son for abandoning his responsibilities and ashamed that he could even think of having relations with a secretary. What was he thinking! Oma was kind and understanding toward Mother but, as usual, offered her no financial assistance or support other than words. Oma took Klaus and me to Verden to live with her and Annenie until Mother found a job and settled her affairs with Vati—which included a highly emotionally charged custody struggle over Klaus and me.

Although the divorce was not contested, the legal tussle in court over Klaus and me raged on for five months. The argument was complicated by the fact that the Ritters wanted to keep us in Germany, but no family member was willing to take care of BOTH of us permanently. According to the United States' Constitution we were American citizens since we were born on U.S. soil. Germany is called *Vaterland* (fatherland), and since our father was German, Klaus and I were also considered Germans. The court said we should be separated. Mother could take one of us, and Vati could take the other child. This was all ridiculous since, obviously, Vati would be out of the country most of the time, and Irmgard, in no uncertain terms, voiced her strong objection to taking either of us. Oma and Annenie said they would take only one child. The judge declared Mother could chose either Klaus or me and return to America and leave the other child in Germany in the care of the grandmother. Mother engaged legal counsel from a German lawyer, Dr. G. Matthaei (Georgesplatz Eleven, Hamburg), who was sympathetic to foreigners and Jews trying to leave the country. I guess it was the only time in Mother's life that she raised her voice, but she said she literally screamed at the judge and told him that she had never done anything in her life except love and take care of her children and support her husband, and she would never, never give up either one of her children. Mother had plenty of documentation and witnesses to prove that she had been the major breadwinner during most of the marriage, how she had been abandoned and worked to keep us with her, and how she had intervened in getting Vati his current military position.

The judge was persuaded by documents, testimony, and Mother's unyielding determination to hold us tight. With Dr. Matthaei's assistance, the judge granted full custody of both Klaus and me to our mother with unrestricted visitation rights for the Ritters. The caveat, however, was that we were to remain in Germany. I might add that it was a good thing for the judge to grant Mother the custody. Losing us was not an option for her. I believe she would have killed anyone in her way or died trying. Mother never lacked in gratitude toward the judge, and until her death, she consistently said that she swore by the German courts and their courage to move against an officer of the German military in favor of an American citizen. My father said to mother in court, "To you, my darling, I've been a rat."

Sometime during her early years of employment, Mother had to provide notarized documentation that she was of Aryan lineage. In the scribbled memo, it looks like she took quick notes to send the necessary information to her sister Annie in Alabama. Fortunately, Mother had the habit of jotting her thoughts on scrap paper before putting her penmanship to the final letter. The reverse side of the memo merely has details of her ancestry sufficient to prove her of Aryan blood. These are the instructions to her sister:

Affidavit stating—

1. Degree of relationship to Aurora Ritter (sister & aunt)
2. That they have knowledge of your birth of _____ on (date)_____.
3. That they know your parents and know (names, place, date of birth) them to be of Aryan (non-Jewish) blood.
4. That they knew your grandparents on both sides, (names, places, date of birth) and knew them also to be of non-Jewish blood.
5. That no official vital records were kept by the local authorities prior to—

To be sworn before notary, or other official commissioned to administer oaths.

His seal and signature to be authenticated by appropriate German Consul, Mobile, Ala. (most probably)

Mother immediately made plans for a new start. It was autumn 1937. She contacted the American Women's Club in Hamburg. They helped her with placement and household items and put her in touch with influential Germans regarding employment. With a highly favorable recommendation from the chaplain of the English Church in Hamburg, Rev. L. G. Forrest, Mother was offered a position by C. H. Merricks to teach English at his language school, Sprachenschule Merricks Glockengiesserwall 20, Hamburg 1. Many of her students were Jews fleeing Germany. She was employed at Merricks from 1 November 1937 until her resignation on 31 December 1938. She located an apartment in Hamburg on Heinrich-Barth Strasse Twenty-four—within easy distance of the city center. Through her connections with the American Women's Club, Mother was also able to purchase enough furniture from foreigners returning to their native lands to furnish a small, but convenient and comfortable, ground-floor apartment. She sublet one room in the apartment to a single lady who looked after Klaus and me until we were able to attend kindergarten. Life was slowly taking on some normalcy again, but new issues developed. There were times when our caretaker left me alone in the apartment when she went upstairs to gossip and have coffee with a friend. I was terribly frightened to be left all alone and spent, what seemed like an eternity, hugging the apartment door listening for familiar voices. The door became my surrogate mother whenever I was left alone. The caretaker also told Mother I was strange because I was talking to myself when I played in the sandbox in the backyard. I was so happy to see Mother when she returned home in the evenings that I never said anything about my miserable day. I don't know how she found out, but she didn't waste any time replacing the roomer/caretaker with a kind lady. Mother was my lifeline. I was only happy when I was with her or Klaus or with Oma and Annenie. Weekday mornings, when Mother left for the office, I would go to the front window and press my face on the glass as I stretched and strained to get the last glimpse of her figure as it melted out of sight. Mother said it would break her heart to leave us. In the evenings when she was home again, I forgot all the day's trauma and my spirit became reconstituted. Klaus was much better adjusted to change. He missed his father but generally thought life was a great adventure. Despite the tremendous pain and hardships from the divorce and lack of income, Mother never showed signs of depression or bitterness. She was deeply hurt but gave credit to her White Oak, Alabama, solid family upbringing, pioneer spirit, and strong faith in God for her strength and determination to carry on. With Mother, tomorrow was always a better day. She taught us that negative thoughts retard and delay action; positive thoughts propel action. She always had her priorities in perfect order! Klaus and I were her number one priority. She was grateful to have her children and good health and not much else was of consequence. She was a 100 percent totally devoted parent. We were her life—forever. We had lots of fun together. The three of us became a team. It was almost impossible for Mother to get angry. If things were really rough, she would give us the evil-eye stare, and that was the end. One of my fondest childhood memories at Heinrich-Barth Strasse was eating or slurping spaghetti one at a time. It all began when Mother admonished us for inhaling our long string of spaghetti, but then we lost control as usual. Klaus and I started to giggle, and soon, all three of us were trying to see who could suck the long noodles up the quickest while the butter splattered in our faces. And as usual, we all nearly fell on the floor laughing. Klaus never had trouble finding entertainment for himself. I think it was at this address where he took all the handles off each door and put the handles, plates, and screws into his apron pocket. When he proudly showed them to Mother, she became overwhelmed with the thought of replacing each handle. Mother stretched her mechanical talent when she had to change a light bulb. Her facial expression became so mournful as she explained to Klaus that she didn't know what to do since she didn't know how to put them back. Klaus was about five then. He felt sorry for her and methodically and correctly installed each handle back to the proper door.

RITTER RING

Spying is not an offence, nor immoral as long as one is a patriot and not self-serving. (Translated by K. F. Ritter) Martens: Internationales Recht der Zivilisierten Nationen 2. Bd. S. 506, Berlin 1886. Quoted by Nikolaus Ritter in his book *Deckname Dr. Ranzau*

SEVERAL MONTHS AFTER Mother's divorce was final, Irmgard and Vati were married and dove full swing into espionage operations against Great Britain and the United States. Vati's military rank was now major, and he and Irmgard moved to Hamburg where they lived in a hotel. To strengthen his foreign network communications, Vati employed sailors and ships' crews from the Hamburg-Amerika and North German Lloyd luxury liners sailing between New York and German North Sea ports. He and Irmgard met the agents at their hotel and then walked from there to Vati's office, which was registered under a false name and phony profession. Vati and his acting chief Captain Kurt Burghardt of the navy realized that in order for Vati to establish a solid ground position for his operation, he needed to go to America. Admiral Canaris was concerned that Vati's possible capture would penetrate the mission. However, Vati convinced Canaris that he knew the Americans and their country well and that he could accomplish the mission in the least amount of time. In November 1937, Vati boarded one of the North German Lloyd ships and sailed for New York under his own passport and name using the guise that he was returning to continue working as a textile engineer. He quickly established himself as Alfred Landing and began his search for new agents.

According to his 1972 autobiography, *Deckname Dr. Rantzau* (*Cover Name Dr. Rantzau*), his code-names were Dr. Johnson or Alfred Landing in America, Dr. Reinhardt or Dr. Weber in Holland, and Dr. Jansen in Hungary—countries in which he concentrated his espionage activities throughout most of the war. He was known as Dr. Renken in Germany.

Vati's espionage activities have been documented in dozens of books; a film; *The House on 49nd Street*; as well as the newly opened International Spy Museum in Washington, D.C. Besides his own war memoirs (Deckname Dr. Rantzau [Hamburg: Hoffmann und Campe Verlag, 1972]), numerous articles and documents have appeared in the *New York Times*, German news publications, and the FBI and CIA files. One of the most recent publications—*Counterfeit Hero: Fritz Duquesne, Adventurer and Spy*, by Art Ronnie, published by the Naval Institute Press in 1995—has extensive references and a solid chronology of Vati's "occupation." In his book, Mr. Ronnie devotes a full chapter to Colonel Ritter. Vati hired Fritz Duquesne, who had espionage experience and hated the British, to assist him in his covert activities in America circa 1939. Mother had met Fritz at Uldric Thomson's home in New Jersey in 1931. The Thomsons and Mother and Vati were good friends. The Thomsons were intellectuals and frequently entertained an interesting mix of guests, including Fritz Duquesne. Mr. Thomson invented a device for safely loading artillery shells with TNT. If I remember correctly, Mother said that he did not get his patent in time, and someone stole it from him. Mr. Thomson spent a fortune to get his device back but died in poverty. As was later revealed, Duquesne was an agent during World War II. Vati, however, was not involved in any conspiracy against the United States in 1931. Mother, Klaus, and I visited Mr. Thomson's home in New Jersey when we returned to the United States in 1946.

As Mr. Ronnie describes in his book,

> Ritter—an extraordinary espionage agent who put together the largest spy organization ever assembled in the United States . . . was especially valuable because of a fluency in French and "American" English . . . . The spy ring—known as the Ritter Ring—became the most successful of all his operations, albeit the most notorious and the most famous

following its eventual breakup in a brilliant stroke of counterespionage by the FBI in 1940 and 1941. It was Ritter's agents who stole the Norden bombsight and Sperry gyroscope, two of America's most closely guarded secrets, gaining possession of these instruments years before the United States even knew Germans had them.

Further documentation of Vati's covert activities is found on the Defense Security Service (DSS) Web site copied below.

In the 1920s an American inventor, Carl L. Norden, had developed a device that promised precision high-altitude bombing. The "Norden Bombsight" became America's most important secret. By November 1937, German spies had stolen the complete plans. The theft was part of a large German espionage operation that would be known as the "Ritter Ring" for Colonel Nikolaus Ritter, who directed it from Hamburg. The Norden operation was carried out by Hermann Lang, a 36-year-old native of Germany, now a naturalized U.S. citizen living in a German-American neighborhood in Queens, New York. He worked as an assembly inspector at the Norden plant on Lafayette Street in downtown Manhattan. (Lang evidently considered himself a German patriot and copied the bombsight plans as an act of German patriotism).

Soon, however, the Federal Bureau of Investigation was onto the operation. Another participant in the Ritter Ring was one Fritz Duquesne, an Afrikaner of Huguenot descent, born in 1877 in the Cape Province, and so a witness to the Boer War. By the 1930s, he was a naturalized U.S. citizen, but was willing to spy against the United States if in so doing he would be "working toward the destruction of his hated enemy, England." On June 29, 1941, 23 members of the Ritter Ring—nineteen in New York and four in New Jersey—were arrested in what J. Edgar Hoover termed for Walter Winchell's broadcast that evening "the greatest spy roundup in U.S. history." (On January 2, 1942, 33 members of the German spy ring headed in the U.S. by Fritz J. Duquesne had been sentenced).

Besides the Norden-bombsight mission, he managed to recruit an agent employed at the Sperry Gyroscope Company of Brooklyn; the agent obtained the plans for an advanced automatic pilot device. The Germans saved a lot of reichmarks on R&D and installed a version of the device on Luftwaffe fighters and bombers.

Among Vati's recruits in America were his youngest brother, Hans, and Hans's girlfriend, Else Weustenfeld. Hans had been in America on legitimate business for several years as a representative of the Chase National Bank in Manhattan. He and Else had been living for five years in a brownstone house at 120 Riverside Drive in a common-law arrangement. Else arrived in the United States from Germany in 1927 and became a citizen ten years later. From 1935 until her arrest, she worked as a stenographer and notary public in the law offices of Topken & Farley located in the Whitehall Building at Seventeen Battery Place, which represented the offices of the German Consulate in New York City. According to FBI documents, Ms. Weustenfeld was thoroughly acquainted with the German espionage system and delivered funds to Fritz Duquesne. Else and Hans continued to serve as Vati's contacts until Hans's identity was exposed. From late 1939 to early 1940, Hans "disappeared" by turning up at Mother's sister's (Annie Lee Fenn) family home in Clayton, Alabama. After visiting long enough to cool his trail, Hans resumed his incognito travels by getting "lost" for six to eight months in Mexico. According to the FBI files, Uncle Hans was reputedly functioning as a paymaster for the German intelligence service in Mexico where he was visited by his paramour, Else. By late 1940, Hans was again in America but returned to Germany, according to FBI files, on Jan. 8, 1941, departing from San Francisco, California, for Japan on the SS *Tatuta Maru*. Eventually, he arrived in Germany by way of Russia. Else continued to assist Vati as a go-between with his spy operators until her arrest 1941. She served approximately seven years in prison.

HAMBURG

In the Foreign Service of the Hamburg American Consulate General,
I also ran into inanities: dreary diplomatic wives following redolent
protocol by saying senseless, silly vanities. Many were the
contradictions. Both the French and the English were more arrogant
than the Germans and the Americans. At that period in history, W.
W. II 1939-1945, the English still demanded to be introduced as
British. A. E. Ritter, *Murmurings.* p. 3

HAMBURG WAS A beautiful and interesting city. It is located in northern Germany on the Elbe River and clusters around a lake (the Alster). The Alster is split by a causeway into the Aussenalster (outer Alster) and the much-smaller harbor Binnenalster (inner Alster). The *Alsterpavillon* is much alive with boutiques, cafés, tour boats, and always-seasonal flowers. I have to mention that at the end of each blooming season, the government gardeners would pull up the spent plants within city plots and replant them with the next season's variety. They always laid the previous season's flowers on the sidewalk for pedestrians to collect. After all, the taxpayer paid for these plants.

Within walking distance of the Alster Pavilion was the Rathaus (city hall). The majestic neo-Renaissance Rathaus was built between 1886 and 1897. It is four to five stories high with pointed dormers all around, elaborate, spiked copper roof, and a central tower with balcony. It was on the center balcony of the Rathaus where Adolph Hitler (Germany's chancellor and Führer, 1934-1945) appeared to the crowd gathered on the large square below. The square was called Adolphplatz. As my brother reminds me, the crowd below would chant in unison, "Lieber Führer komm raus; es sieht so nach Regen aus." This means "Dear leader, come on out; it looks like it's going to rain." Basically, the crowd was saying, "Get yourself out here because we're tired of waiting." Eventually, Hitler would march onto the tiny balcony, and the crowd greeted him with the official raised right arm and repeated chants of "Sieg heil!" He presented himself in a formal, almost puppet like manner with staccato movements. We all stretched our right arms up toward him and chanted hail to Hitler, and he would return the salute. This greeting was repeated several times before he began his address. He was a dynamic speaker and could mesmerize his audiences. It was impossible to identify his followers from those of us who were merely going through the motions of pretence. He could not be ignored. His convictions moved the crowd. The Führer bellowed pontifications on and on in his shrill, sometimes trembling, voice. No one dared to leave nor give the appearance of disagreement while he was lecturing. The little I remember of him, he always seemed strung tight and nervous. Then it was over, and he gave his salute again. Not a negative comment was uttered as the crowd dispersed. We only heard him a couple of times in person when we happened to be at the Alster Pavilion or shopping nearby. Mother, Klaus, and I only responded with Sieg Heil! because we were afraid someone might be looking at us and report us for unpatriotic behavior—which could be by anyone, anywhere, anytime. It was not a healthy idea to look agitated, antagonistic, or not to participate in traditional Nazi Party rituals—especially for foreigners. Mother always made sure that we did not distinguish ourselves as foreigners. Despite the fact that the United States still had not entered the war, we were under surveillance and had our mail intercepted and censored.

The rise of the Nazi Party was escalated substantially by Adolf Hitler's dynamic oratory skill and style, which were fueled by his hatred of Communists, Jews and a wimpy German government. As a Lance Corporal in World War I, it infuriated Adolf Hitler that by signing the peace settlement after the war, the Treaty of Versailles, 1919, representatives of the Weimar Republic relinquished much of Germany's major industrial territory, and reduced their military force to 100,000, with no air force and only six navy ships. Also, Germany had to admit full responsibility for starting the war and therefore make huge cash reparations. Basically, Germany was bankrupt and millions of people were without jobs.

The period of German history from 1919 to 1933 is known as the Weimar named after the city of Weimar where a national assembly convened to produce a new constitution after the German monarchy was abolished following the nation's defeat in World War I. Political parties during this time include the Social Democrats, Independent Socialists, Communists, Centre Party (Catholics), Bavarian People's Party, Democrats, People's Party, Economy Party, and the National Socialist party (Nationalsozialists (Nazis)). In 1919 and 1920, there were no elected deputies of the Nazi Party. The Social Democrats were in control. By 1924, out of 472 electorates, the Nazi Party had only 32 electorates, and the Social Democrats, 131. By September 1930, out of a total of 577 electorates the Social Democrats had 143 electorates and the Nazis 107. Nazi membership in the 1920's was about 2000.

Adolf Hitler continued to nurture his cause, which was to return Germany to its original political and economic power without acquiescing to the terms of the 1919 Versailles treaty. In his 1968 book *The Rise and Fall of the Third Reich* William Shirer writes that, Adolf Hitler lectured to "60,000 persons in Brandenburg, to nearly as many in Potsdam, and that same evening to 120,000 massed in the giant Grünewald Stadium in Berlin while outside an additional 100,000 heard his voice by loudspeaker." He appealed to the hungry and weary public's emotions by declaring himself the only hope for the future.

Yet when Germans went to the polls to elect a new president, Field Marshall Paul von Hindenburg won the majority votes by 53 percent while Hitler carried nearly 37 percent. However, because of Adolph Hitler's relentless campaigning, he was able to drastically increase his popularity, and by January 1933 the Nazi Party membership swelled to nearly 2.5 million. Based on his popularity Hitler requested that Hindenburg appoint him chancellor. When von Hindenburg died a year and a half later, Adolf Hitler combined his chancellorship with the presidency thereby making himself head of the government and the Nazi Party. He changed his title to Führer (one who leads).

Mother's foreign accent drew attention to us during discourse. It was a bit of a novelty to see foreigners about. Uttering the phonetic pronunciation of vowels, making the guttural r sound, and placing the tongue just right for the ch sounds in the German language were particularly difficult for her. Klaus and I would frequently tease Mother and make her practice the sounds. Of course, German was our native language. Mostly, I have good memories growing up in Germany—war and all. I believe that it is due to the fact that I had fully depended on and trusted Mother. I was convinced that she would never leave us or let anything bad happen to us. And she never let us down!

Our pleasures and appreciation for beauty came primarily from the exposure to family art and heirlooms within our and our grandmother's home. Besides dodging bombs, we had access to nature walks in the country, frequent outdoor concerts, the theater, museums, botanical and zoological parks, and lots of indoor and outdoor games.

Hamburg had a wonderful *Tierpark* (zoo) called Hagenbeck. It was considered the best in Germany and offered an exceptionally pleasant respite for us children from pavement life. Of particular pleasure to Mother was one of Hagenbeck's singing birds. Each time Mother heard the music from *Cavalleria Rusticana*, "Intermezzo Sinfonico" by Pietro Mascagni, she stopped whatever she was doing and said, "A bird in Hagenbeck whistles that tune." It means "Er hat mir auf die Shulter gekuessed [He kissed me on the shoulder]." Planten und Blomen was another favorite retreat. Planten und Blomen was an arboretum near the train station. Planten und Blomen is *plattdeutsch* for plants and flowers. "Plattdeutsch" (literally, "flat," or "low," in German) is a regionally used German dialect. We took long walks during specific flowering seasons in Planten und Blomen. Besides the many trees, shrubs, and flowerbeds, the park had a massive water garden. The fountain was electronically connected to a sound system and included a dozen or more waterspouts that shot out of the reflecting pool. The height and pattern of each water jet was determined by the volume and tempo of each note—keeping time with whatever arrangement was playing over the loudspeakers. At night, different colored lights in the pool projected upward through the waterspouts and danced to the beat of the music against the dark sky. It was awesome and fascinating. We often sat in the outdoor café nearby. Mother enjoyed a cold glass of beer, and Klaus and I had juice—with an occasional taste of the foam on Mother's beer. This ambience was festive and deeply enriching to me as a child. Being surrounded by an environment that appealed to so many of my senses all at once was like living in a fairy tale world.

No one should ever think that children don't enjoy glamour or beauty. The excitement of getting dressed in our finest clothes to attend an evening play or concert is remembered fondly. I can still clearly recall my navy blue silk dress with a red belt that tied in front. The belt was wide with appliqués of flowers and animals. I still have the belt. The luxury of these rare evenings at the grand theater, with its warm lights and elegant crowds, was meaningful to me and continues to decorate my memory. In October, we celebrated the Laterne Fest (Lantern Festival). Children paraded in parks and on the street at night with beautifully adorned and cut paper lanterns. They were about the size of a basketball hanging from a stick. We had to hold the lanterns still since they were always lit by a single candle inside. For lustful folks, there is the famous Reeperbahn— like the French Quarter in New Orleans—or more like an active government-controlled red-light district. Hamburg had something to offer all yearnings.

The downside for Mother, naturally, was the craving for intimacy. She had dozens of wonderful friends. And of course, Klaus and I were naive enough to think that she didn't need any company except us. On rare occasions, she mentioned hurtful isolated experiences. One such time was when Klaus had a high fever, and she had to rush him to the nearest clinic. She said it was late evening and bitterly cold on a dreary day with deep snow on the ground when she bundled Klaus and me up and carried us to the doctor. On the way back from the doctor, she ran into Vati and Irmgard, huddled together arm in arm, enjoying the obvious pleasure and comfort of each other's companionship. It pains me for her, even now, to recall this scene. It seems like the more hurt she endured, the more determined she became to survive and devote her life to our family. In her book, *Murmurings*, she writes:

> Love without an object shrivels like a flower betrayed by an early frost. How can one live without it? Without love? Without its total commitment? Acceptance finally comes. Substitutes are possible. The scars of bitter grief are like unto battle stripes, marks of a fight to attain identity. My children were fulfilling for me. They gave to me strength, understanding, sympathy. One never loses the past but one's perspective changes—broadens.

In one of her 1940 letters to a dear friend Emily Frojen, who left Germany before the United States entered the war, she explains, "Since work I *must*, I have firmly chosen to go through life alone and to use my ambitions alone for the kiddies."

For the rest of Mother's life, not for an instant did she ever waver from that promise.

With many letters from both Germany and the United States highly supporting her good character and work ethics, she applied for a position with the American Consulate. I've selected one such letter of recommendation below to include in the text:

WILLIAM KARLIN

COUNSELOR AT LAW   (Enclosure no 1. to Dispatch No. 465
291 Broadway   dated April 6, 1939 from
New York   The Consulate General, Hamburg.)

TELEPHONE WORTH Z-0237-0255

To the American Consul,
Hamburg, Germany.

Honorable Sir:

This is to certify that I have been personally well acquainted with Mrs. Aurora Ritter for over six years. I have known her professionally and socially and have known an appreciable number of other people who know her. Some of these persons are highly placed in the professional and business world of New York City. Her reputation among them is and always has been excellent for reliability, good moral character, as well as excellent ability. At one time she was the chief administrator of a private hospital in New York City which prospered under her management.

Mrs. Ritter is a fine specimen of American culture and civilization. Her devotion to the cause of American democracy is unquestioned. I have no hesitations in recommending her for faithful service at the American Consulate.

respectfully yours,
William Karlin

In the spring of 1939, Mother joined the American Consulate in Hamburg as a permanent staff member of the foreign service of the United States. She was not only directly in charge of the American Consulate's shipping department but was also thoroughly acquainted with the operations of the different consular branches. Working in the shipping department was a highlight in Mother's career. She repeatedly expressed to us the pleasure of her position at the consulate. She became acquainted with many of the foreign shipping lines and their employees, and it was not uncommon for them to bring her gifts from all over the world. In 1940, a year after Mother was hired, Mr. Alfred Ray Thomson was made consul general. Mr. Thomson became one of Mother's most loyal and trusted friends.

For a year now, Adolf Hitler had already begun his expansion into German-speaking territories under the pretext that he wanted to unite all lands where German is spoken. France and Britain watched and waited. Hitler annexed Austria in March 1939 and made a pact with Russia to divide Poland between them. It was these threats to Poland that finally convinced Britain and France to stand firm and declare war on Germany on September 1, 1939. The German population was never aware of Hitler's aggressions and prejudices. The government-controlled media only broadcast and printed what was specifically programmed to enlighten and educate the general population on a utopian Germany. No one knew. In a free society, it is difficult to comprehend that the average pedestrian had not a clue regarding World War II atrocities. But how would they know without a free press? No one dared express doubt or rumor. I'm sure Mother had intimate friends with whom she exchanged suspicious ideas, but that is a risky business. Whoever controls the media controls the minds and thoughts of the people. Above all, Adolf Hitler made the radio his weapon of choice to prejudice the German public. He was a prime example of a micromanager. Besides being eager to command most of Europe, he wanted to create and develop what he conceived to be a genetically superior race. This concept was not unique to Adolf Hitler. The American Consultative Committee was appointed at the first International Congress of Eugenics in 1912. Adolph Hitler corresponded with American authors of the eugenics theory. Prominent members of the first committee included Alexander Graham Bell, Vernon Lyman Kellogg, and Henry Fairfield Osborn, its president. After going through several name changes, the society is now called Society for the Study of Social Biology. Their journal's purpose today is "to further knowledge of the biological and sociocultural forces affecting human populations and their evolution." How did Adolph Hitler conceive the idea that he alone could determine the worth of human life? Was it his syphilitic brain, sexual frigidity, or chronic insomnia that threw him into paranoiac rages? Although never proven with certainty, rumors to that affect were widespread.

Inner and Outer Alster in Hamburg

Rathausmarkt

VATI

It was difficult to reconcile myself to
the idea of working against the country which
I loved best next to my own native land. Nikolaus A. Fritz Ritter

IRMGARD WAS PREGNANT and moved into her grandparents' home in Hamburg. She was an only child, and both her parents and her grandfather were deceased. She and her grandmother lived in the family homestead—a multistory, elegantly furnished Victorian stone house on the prominent Rothenbaumchaussee, approximately four blocks from where Mother, Klaus, and I lived. Having secured his spy network in America in only one month, Vati returned to Hamburg in December 1937. He continued his operation from his Hamburg office and moved in to the von Klitzing home with his wife and daughter, Karen. Vati had unrestricted visitation rights to Klaus and me, and since we lived so nearby, he frequently walked to our apartment to pick us up, and then the three of us would spend the day at Irmgard's house. The von Klitzing home was impressive with its beveled glass front door and wrought-iron outer gate. Inside, the high ceiling of the immense entry hall went all the way to the third floor. Heavy wooden banisters encircled the space over the foyer in the center of the home. The second floor is where the parlor, dining room, and bedrooms were. Vati and Irmgard lived on the second floor. Irmgard's grandmother disapproved of Vati. Also, she was bitter and angry with her granddaughter for taking a man away from his family. Klaus and I rarely interfaced with her, but on those occasions, she was pleasant. Vati was noticeably proud of Irmgard's elegant home, social status, and political clout. It was Irmgard's nature to be correct, pleasant, but somewhat aloof. Vati was fully attentive to us when we were with him, and Irmgard supported our relationship. Vati was playful and fun to be with. We considered him a master magician. He made coins appear and disappear. (Unfortunately, this talent didn't transfer to his real life.) He flipped the money around in his hand, rubbed it hard and said *hocus-pocus filibus,* and it was gone. Then he told us to go look for it. We searched all over him— pockets, vest, sleeves, and shoes—but never found it. Then he told us to look around the room until we finally found it under some vase or ashtray or in his favorite brown leather chair (which Mother had bought for him). We never ceased to be amazed at his genius. We were totally stumped as to how a coin could have slipped past us and flown across the room without us seeing it. I think we were adults before we found out that he had hidden money under specific objects in the room before we arrived. What a letdown. During these and all visits, I considered Vati more like an uncle. I loved him, but I never could think of him as my father. My bond was only with my mother. I believe Klaus was much more in need of a close male relationship and a role model, of course. I'm sure we both were affected by not having a father in the home, but he provided almost no financial or real emotional support for his children. To me, he was a good sperm donor. The gene pool is good—healthy, intelligent, and talented in music and art.

In the fall of 1939, Vati's activities in the Abwehr were intensified by the hiring of a new agent to be trained as a radio operator and stationed in New York. William Sebold came highly recommended to my father after a scrutinizing investigation into his background by the Gestapo. With Sebold acting as the focal point in New York for transmitting American and British activities to Germany, the Ritter Ring became so successful that other German spy groups asked to use Sebold as their contact man in America. This was most likely the downfall of the Ritter Ring since Sebold eventually contacted the American consul in Cologne and became a double agent. Unaware and believing that his organization was running smoothly, in 1941, Vati was assigned to continue espionage work out of Budapest, Hungary, where he met Captain Laszlo and Count von Almaszy, an expert and surveyor of the Sahara Desert. Being intrigued by the necessity to help Egypt free itself from Britain's dominance, Vati devised a bold plan to recruit the chief of the general staff of the Egyptian army, E Masri Pasha, who had been dismissed by the British. According to the *The Foxes of the Desert* by Paul Carell, and by Vati's own account to us, Pasha hated the British as much as the Germans and agreed to be airlifted by the Germans to Germany to help the Egyptian cause for freedom. In the spring of 1941, Vati and his special commandos of ten, including Count von Almaszy, obtained two Heinkel He III aircraft. These were light bomber planes also sometimes called mosquito bombers. One plane was used for lookout while the other would land and retrieve the General. Just prior to takeoff to fetch General Pasha, Vati's team received word that General Pasha had been in a car accident. The next attempt to pick Pasha up was in June 7, 1941. The two He IIIs arrived at the appointed time and rendezvous point, but no one was there. After fifteen minutes, they returned to their home base without the general. It was learned that the general decided to fly to the rendezvous point, and his airplane crashed into a tree. He was captured by the Egyptians but "allowed" to escape, because they had sympathy with his cause. General Pasha continued to transmit information, but never made another attempt to defect.

Vati's next assignment was to stage a special intelligence operation for Field Marshal Erwin Rommel, who held the command of the Deutsches Afrika Korps. Rommel was sent to aid Germany's Italian ally in their struggle against the British. He requested reliable intelligence information regarding the British base in Egypt. The mission was to drop two agents and a motorcycle sixty miles from Cairo so they could drive into the city and collect valuable data from the Egyptian and British communities. Again, Vati deployed two He IIIs for this mission, one to stay in the air to provide aerial observation, the other to deliver the motorcycles and the two agents. When the pilot on the He carrying the agents approached the desert sand, the inexperienced pilot panicked and refused to land because he was seeing obstructions on the undulating ground when, in fact, the late-day sun had silhouetted pebbles into tall shadows, resembling boulders. He tried and tried again, spending too much fuel in the air, while the crew screamed at him that he was just seeing shadows. However, he refused to land, and much to the consternation of Vati and crew, the mission had to be aborted. On their return to base, they ran out of fuel. Night had already come upon them, and they agreed to crash-land in the Mediterranean Sea. One of the crew was killed; the others were able to crawl onto the cockpit and inflate a rubber dinghy only large enough for four. The other two had to hang on. Vati was credited with saving the life of one of the crew members when he pushed the dazed man out of the craft. Vati's right arm was crushed. They were twelve hours in the water. They paddled all night and on until the following midday when the tide brought them to shore. After an incredulous march through the hot desert, almost dying of thirst, they reached an Arab village and were rescued by the Desert Rescue Squadron. Vati was flown back to Germany and hospitalized.

Our family was informed about the He's crash and the broken arm, and that Vati was hospitalized somewhere in Germany. After that, we lost communication with Vati. We never saw or heard news of Vati until after the war. Whenever we asked our grandmother or aunt we were told that he was missing. Later, we learned that he was assigned to desk duty in the Luftwaffe (air force) after his hospitalization and rose to the rank of colonel. After the war, Vati confirmed that he was made head of air defense for major cities in Germany.

There were as many or more failures in Vati's illustrious career than accomplishments. The *London Telegraph* offered several accounts of his failures that were challenged by family members. Who knows for sure? As damaging and deadly as espionage work is, I believe there is a certain play involved. It's a game, and the players aren't always as interested in the patriotic objective as they are in the thrill of the challenge.

Vati, 1940.

Vati (left) returning from mission in Junkers JU-52

WAR

It was queer that I had to find my clue as to how to get on with my life from a bombing war on the European continent rather than from my family—or from a preacher. How to account for suffering to a child is not easy when no one knows the answers. I distain religions of fear. That is demeaning to love. Before God, I had just one duty as a parent. That was to see that my children had a happy childhood tucked under their jackets. I tried! I tried!!

A. E. Ritter, *Murmurings.* p. 209

BY SPRING 1940 THE air raids were escalating and hitting closer to Hamburg. At this time, our daily routine was only interrupted by infrequent air attacks. Bombing raids from the British usually came in the evening or at night and the sirens gave us warning. One long, up-and-down waving sound for warning that enemy planes were heading in our direction and quick bursts of the siren for imminent danger and to seek shelter. When the planes had passed over, we heard the all-clear signal, which was one long extended sound. Sometimes the bombers turned around or abruptly changed course and flew back in our direction. The sirens usually let us know. Whenever they flew over us we never knew if we were the intended target. I remember the great care we had to take each evening to pull shades, shutters, and drapes over our windows to black out all light visible from outside. The city had to lie in total darkness each evening. If one little stream of light peeked through the shades, either a private citizen or the police would knock on the door and request total blackout.

On one occasion when Vati was walking Klaus and me back home from a visit with him, he spotted a tiny streak of light coming from an upper floor window of an apartment building. He dashed up and informed the occupants that their light was visible from the street. We saw the light go out before he came back to the sidewalk. It's amazing that one thin light beam can be detected from the sky and will expose the location of an entire city. To combat darkness, the enemy (at this date the British) projected flares from the planes into the sky to illuminate the ground below for target identification. We called the flares Christmas Trees in Germany because they were little multi-colored explosions that remained suspended over the shadowy city like lingering firecrackers before they spread out and fade. It was a fascinating and exciting spectacle. *Schadenfreude*, a sad joy, as the Germans might say. For a few minutes we became transfixed as we tilted our heads back and gazed upward into an animated sound version of Vincent van Gogh's *Starry Night*—all along forgetting that we are the target of this terrible splendor. The bombs came next, of course. "Not too close," we hope. I was frightened, but it was not uncommon for people to gawk at the sky and be engrossed with the eerie black-blue haze, which illuminated the outline of buildings and tips of cathedrals and towers—all silhouetted against the busy war sky. It was like someone turned one dim light bulb on in a warehouse. The German *scheinwerfers* (searchlights) crisscrossed the sky, scanning the dark void in search for enemy planes. When the roaming, back-and-forth patterns of the powerful light beacons spotted their target, the German antiaircraft military went into action aiming their long barrel guns into the bomber formations. Next, we heard the booms from the cannons as they shot their ground flak toward moving targets in the sky traced by the spotlights. These guns could reach targets twenty-six thousand feet away. Germans also used twenty-millimeter and the deadly eighty-eight-millimeter cannons. According to Paul Tibbets's book *Return of the Enola Gay*, the ammunition in the eighty-eights was effective on bombers flying as high as twenty-five thousand feet. It could blow an airplane out of the sky with one shot and it could be fired at a rate of forty rounds a minute. Another antiaircraft defense was the Bofors-type ground weapon, which simply shot a wall of exploding steel shrapnel into the path of the airplanes. This was used for lower-flying aircraft. Also, Germans made use of the barrage balloons which would hinder invasion of low-flying aircraft. Barrage balloons, like helium filled blimps, dotted our neighborhood. These heavy gray blimps were tethered by steel cables and could be lowered and raised up to 10,000 feet, to deter enemy planes. The idea was to impede bombing accuracy and to force the flight path of the bombers into ground-based artillery. Even the tethering cables were strong enough to inflict damage to low flying aircraft.

A bombing mission by the British and Americans was considered successful if they lost no more than 10 percent of their fleet. Blinding pilots with powerful search lights was often as affective as bringing planes down with cannon fire. Some nights, the air raids went on for hours—bombs and cannons, not all from our city. We could hear war for miles. We dreaded full-moon nights—especially if the sky was clear and the moon had an aura around it. It was certain that such natural illumination would provide superior visibility for crews of combat airplanes, and our angst increased as the night drew longer. Waiting heightened our fear as we dreaded the drone of aircraft engines, whistling bombs, and the big-bang finale. The converse was true too of course. Hazy or overcast nights promised relative assurance that we would sleep undisturbed.

The correspondence that follows is from Mother to her friend Emily Frojen. I believe Mother met Emily through her husband, who was on the staff of the consulate in Hamburg. The letter is several pages long, but I think it sets the mood for what life was like for her in Hamburg, in May 1940.

May 17, 1940
At the Office-

Dear Emily and children,

I was so happy to receive your letter and to know that at least you are physically well that it has taken me some weeks to return to normal thinking. Not that I have lost my sense of humor exactly, but in the midst of so much war and dismal disaster, it is almost overwhelming to read of the peace and sunshine that still is felt in other parts of the world. Then too I had feared that all was not well with you. I don't know why such an idea possessed me. I should know by this time that you are more than capable of keeping the proverbial wolf from the door and of holding yourself in the pink. Suffice it to say that each day I think frequently of you and wish for your return.

The first letter that you wrote was emptied entirely of all contents and only the envelope was turned over to me from the "Zensur Stelle." My complaint fell on empty ears. Germany said that England had done it and vice versa. I presumed from the nature of the envelope that you had enclosed something for the kiddies. The second letter came through rather promptly. That is typical of the mail today. Many letters go hopelessly astray, others are delayed indefinitely, and the third may break all speed records. I recently received my birthday letter from my family written in September, and Christmas letters are still arriving.

I enjoyed your description of Christmas in California, and the school experiences of the children. It is wonderful for all of you if you can accept it as an "Übergangszeit" (transition period), but that is more easily said than done. Uncertainty is the worst thing I know—even worse than failure and tragedy, and *I should know* because it has been my fate to live in the midst of it for almost 2 score years. No, not exactly so bad. My own home life in the sunny south was rather ideal as I see it now. Unfortunately, however, we fallible human beings never realize that we are happy until it has passed into a memory. But as Henry Ford once said in a public statement: "All that I personally own of any value is my experience, and that cannot be taken away." So one should not complain it seems of having one's fund of experience added to. Complaints do not stimulate progress any more than a foolish credulity does. History has proven to us that all things will pass when their purpose has been served. A POOR COMFORT to you, my dear, in your divided home-life but it shall not last forever, and if America stays out of the fight I predict that all the Frojens will celebrate next Christmas together at Schluteerstrasse 6 in Hamburg. Even before then I shall have the flags flying for your return. If Germany succeeds in gaining Belgium why then I believe that all of Europe is facing a N. S. regime. It is more than difficult to pass a valuable opinion at this time but certainly for the minute it appears to be favorable for Germany. Wilhelm Busch is to me about the finest German humorist and philosopher the country has ever known. His proverb was always—"Erstens, kommt es anders—Zweitens, als man denkt." (Things never turn out the way you think). So the best thing after all is *just not think.*

Of all things I shall be interested in hearing you compare the pros and cons of American and German education and training. That is for me at present a tremendously important subject. How do your children compare with the children from the same type of American homes? Has their European school life been an asset or hindrance? I've always thought that a German understood thoroughness better than we and that the children were trained early to know how to think. Am I wrong or right? If wrong then I shall exert all efforts possible to get a transfer to the States.

'Tis sweet of you Emily to encourage me in all the things that I dream of doing but cannot. I see no plausible reason why I should not be able to advance in the Foreign Service except that perhaps soon we shall have no foreign service representatives. I fear against fear that America shall try to enter this fight and then, of course, I shall be notified only 24 hrs. previous to my departure from the country. I must give 3 months notice on the apartment and since I could not do so everything would remain standing. Will Washington be able to give us employment? I doubt it—hence again the beginning for yours truly. I am glad to have your sister's address and to feel that I cannot lose complete sight of you and the children. I shall always want to know where you are and how you are and to follow the success of the children. Likewise I shall note here for you the permanent address of my eldest sister—Mrs. William Fenn, Clayton, Alabama. It is a one-horse town of only 2 thousand inhabitants but they are all as proud as peacocks down there, and my sister is a jewel. I'd love to have you run by to see her on some of your cross-country tours. Otherwise you may write to me in care of the Department of State, Washington. They will, of course, have a line-up on me as long as I remain in their services.

V. C. Davis and Miss Jones were unofficially engaged at the time that they left Hamburg but he has been transferred to China and the last that we heard of Jones she was still in Washington. I never was keen on Jones myself, and for the simple reason that she insisted upon being the whole show and used her proficient charms only to that end. She was ever so friendly to me in the service here but somehow I never took her attention as a really serious gesture. I even felt that she had something to do with Keblinger's prolongation of my trial. Immediately after her resignation I was made permanent. She was a man's type and concentrated upon the art, but I don't think that I felt any jealousy of her. Since work I *must* I have firmly chosen to go through life alone and to use my ambitions alone for the kiddies.

Both children are well and have grown to be quite large. We've all had a siege of colds-again and again. The winter was the worst that Hamburg has known for over 100 years and we all were cut in the coal allowance to an uncomfortable extent. I can't describe to you just how frightfully we froze. Even now in late May the weather is sharp and biting. Only woolen dresses are used and fur coats still popular.

May 22, 1940

Five days later and I'm back trying to tell you all about the land of the Huns again. So much has happened in the meantime. One cannot grasp it all without a swirling of the head. The most recent excitement was the sudden swooping down on us by the English and the death of 33 Hamburgers— mostly private citizens and private homes were hit. Hamburg and St. Pauli were the worst points of attack. The flight lasted for over 4 hours and there was not doubting the seriousness of it. The sirens did not seem to be in order because the first bombing started before 10: in the evening and it was after 12: before we were warned. In the meantime I sat helplessly over Katharine cooling her forehead and hoping that the rumbling could be thunder and lightning and realizing that it was not. We went in the air raid room at about 12:30 and remained there till 3: but we knew well that we were not safe. It was a frightful night. The next evening the bombing was repeated by England but Hamburg was better prepared to fight and few lives were lost.

Our section of the city was untouched and in so far as I know, your lovely home is patiently awaiting your early return. And if America does not enter the fight, I predict an early Armistice and an early return to normal living conditions. Even if America comes in—there's nothing for us to win, and I'm afraid we'd all lose together. I absolutely agree with Lindbergh that our problems lie at home. What do you say? I shall be happy to hear you say it when all has passed.

War can be as fascinating as it is dreadful. For me, the most frightening characteristics of the war were the overhead bombings. Mother was always convinced that her mother was near and protected us from harm. She was amazingly calm. And as I mentioned before, Klaus was more enamored with the adventure of it all. During an air raid, most people were tense, sitting or standing pensively, rigid in some basement, commercial shelter, or backyard dugout assessing their proximity to their location of the bomb's whistle and explosion. If we had electricity, the lights would soon flicker and then go off. Sometimes we had emergency lighting; other times we sat for hours in total darkness, waiting for the bombs to obliterate us or for another chance at life. As the waves of close formations of dozens of bomber squadrons approached our city, we concentrated on the incessant humming of the planes' engines—like a steady swarm of giant bees— that started in the distance and grew louder and louder as the drone of engines came overhead. Then we all stopped talking and just listened and held our breath, hoping the planes would pass over and fade away. When the bombers keep flying into the distance, the calm after the terror is almost like a born-again experience.

If Hamburg was selected as general target area for the night, we listened with bated breath as the whistling bombs dropped closer and louder overhead in our direction. These bombs weighed anywhere from five hundred to two thousand pounds. One raid could drop more than 150 tons of explosives in one night and an additional dozens of tons of incendiaries. Once we heard the BANG, we exhaled.

We were still in one piece but wondered which of our neighbors was now dead and where the next one would strike. The adults in the cellar always calculated the name of the street, church, or housing development where they thought the blast might have occurred. Sometimes, as the bombs hailed down, folks in the basement would say, "That one's going to be close" or "This is going to hit down the block from us" or "That sounded like it hit near Mr. Schmidt's house." You could also tell if the bomb hit a building or the ground. The thuds were different. If we heard a bomb's whistle but no bang, we knew the bomb didn't explode, and our neighborhood was in danger. A detonation team would have to come and degauss the bomb—hopefully before the fascinated public went sightseeing. If we were forced into a public shelter, it was much the same. Children might whimper, but it was strange. I never heard babies screaming. There was an acceptance among the crowd while we all just waited. Many people preferred to hover near the shelter entrance, afraid of getting trapped.

On bad nights, as repeated waves of bomber-squadron reinforcements unloaded their tons of explosives on our city, I just squeezed my eyes shut and huddled close to Mother. One felt like a sitting duck with no place to hide.

We all became good wartime listeners. Our ears were sensitized to sky and ground noises. We were able to tell the difference between British and German planes. The sound waves of the tight bomber formations of British and American planes produced a repetitive, quick, reverberating high-low hum while the German planes caused a solid, steady droning sensation overhead.

As war progressed in Germany, so did the number of air raids and their duration. Total exhaustion—emotional and physical—followed. If we were lucky, there still was time for sleep. Sleep came immediately. It was so good to be alive that life in-between attacks was concentrated and pleasant. I never thought about being scared of bombings until the siren sounded. War years for us were exciting. Children are easily bored and war provided a perverse sort of entertainment. We never knew what the next day's program would be. As the nursery rhyme goes, "When it was good, it was very good and when it was bad it was horrid."

SUMMERS

*My children are honestly the most treasured mainstay
in my life. Their problems are my problems and their
victories, mine. There is something almost mystical about
this intricate link.* A. E. Ritter, *Murmurings.* p. 22

Verden an der Aller

MOST OF OUR summers were spent in Verden an der Aller with
our grandmother and aunt, Tante Annenie. Mother sent us on the
train with name tags and "destination Verden" around our necks
and Oma and Annenie met us at the train station with great
anticipation and excitement. It seemed like we were on the train for
an eternity, but I think it was only about two to three hours before we
arrived in Verden. The four of us either walked or took a horse and
buggy to Oma's house, which was on the other side of the city on the
Aller River. A bit of Verden history is worth mentioning here.

The name of the town comes from "furt" (ford) and "fähre" (ferry)
and was first noted on a Teutonic map around AD 150. In the year
810, the colony is named Ferdi in Saxony. After the Thirty Years'
War, the bishopric Verden and the archbishopric Bremen belonged
as dukedoms to Sweden and, in 1719, to Hanover. During the
Napoleonic Wars, Verden belonged to Prussia, to the Kingdom of
Westphalia in 1810, and to the Empire of France in 1811-1813. It
belonged to Prussia in 1866. Since the reformation of today's federal
republic after World War II, 1946, Verden belongs to the county of
Lower Saxony. As Verden has a clerical past as a bishopric, many

sacred buildings and reminders of the Middle Age in the old part of the town make up a pictorial townscape.

Today, Verden is the center of animal husbandry in Lower Saxony. Based on the horse auctions, Verden is also called Reiterated (Riders town). According to the European Mastership of Dressage in August 1997, Verden has become quite popular for its wonderful turf areas. Today, horse lovers and visitors from around the globe come to enjoy the meadows and riding stables of Verden.

Verden is typical of any old European historical village with brick houses, high pointed slate roofs, all clustered together and store fronts lining the brick sidewalks dangling their names and advertisements on placards suspended on wrought-iron brackets above the doorways. Its quaint buildings, old, narrow, cobblestone alleys, and its location on the Aller River made it an attractive respite for city dwellers from Bremen, Hamburg and Hannover. As we neared Oma's home, the area turned more residential with wrought iron-fenced, well manicured yards and larger houses set back from the street, surrounded by tidy english gardens. No one had lawns or grass. My grandparents' home was a three-story, light gray stucco house that belonged to the college where my grandfather had been president. My grandfather had built seven well landscaped, meandering garden terraces down to the Aller River behind the house. At the end of the terrace trail, just before the water, was a little alcove retreat with an iron and wood bench, chairs and a round table. The front yard had a four-foot black wrought-iron fence and gate separating the house from the sidewalk lined with Maple trees. A decorative blue-and-yellow-glazed ceramic-tile walkway led to the main side entrance. The house had a large cheerful veranda in front, overlooking a plush english garden of flowerbeds and herbs maintained by my aunt. Today, nearly sixty years later, when I visit my neighbor's garden and inhale the fresh and tender fragrance of her boxwoods, I'm instantly beamed to the scent of boxwoods in my grandmother's garden and visualize my aunt bending over her flowerbeds. Klaus and I loved visiting Verden. My grandmother and aunt were at home all the time. Oma received Opa's pension, and my aunt was paid by the German government to take care of her mother. Even after Oma died, Annenie continued to receive a pension just as if she had been employed by an organization. They lived elegantly and comfortably. They sublet the second floor for extra income. The spacious attic was full of dusty secrets. We never went there alone, but sometimes when Annenie was searching for something upstairs, we had time to marvel at her extensive and exceptionally well-preserved butterfly and dried wildflower collections stored in the attic.

Our typical day in Verden began by climbing out of our beds and getting into bed with Oma and Annenie for our morning puppet play. They picked up clumps of bed sheet in each hand and fluffed them up like puppets and began a conversation. We always interacted with the puppets as if they were real. Next we washed, dressed, and had breakfast on the veranda. Germans usually cook only one hot meal a day. That's the noon meal. Breakfast is bread, butter, jam, coffee, hot chocolate, boiled eggs, and sometimes a meat spread. Our life at my grandmother's was formal but fun. The table always looked elegant with hand-embroidered tablecloth, fine china, and silver. Coffee and hot chocolate were only poured from a china pot and kept warm with a *café mütze* (a quilted cap or tea cozy). Our bread was usually coarse black bread. Butter was scarce. But schmaltz, the commercially rendered bacon fat with salt, tasted pretty good. When we had finished eating, Annenie would say, "Now you can make your coffee cake." This meant that we could have a tiny bit of coffee in the cup, fill it partially with milk, and crumble black bread into it. We packed it down tightly with a spoon and turned the cup upside down onto our plate. Then, we'd sprinkle the clump of coffee-soaked bread with sugar and ate our coffee cake. It really wasn't that good, but the idea of playing with our food at the table and going through all that procedure was fun, and we always ate our little "cupcakes." If we ever spilled our chocolate on the tablecloth, Annenie moved all the dishes and napkins aside to analyze the spill. We discussed the shape of the brown spot as if it were a Rorschach test. After breakfast, the next order of business was laundry, yard work, or a bit of house cleaning and starting lunch. Klaus and I usually played outside or "helped" Annenie in the ground-floor basement with the laundry. Tablecloths were mostly spot cleaned. Linen napkins (paper napkins were an extravagance we couldn't afford) and sheets were washed once a week and hung out to dry. All other bedding and rugs were hung on a line and beaten with a special tool that looked like a tennis racket.

Even drapes and mattresses were dragged outside to air. Mother regularly carried our Oriental rugs outdoors, turned them right side down in the snow, and beat the dirt and sand into the snow. I was always amazed by the amount of *schmutz* absorbed by the white snow afterward.

Klaus and I built castles in the sandbox at Oma's and made mud pies under the enormous blue spruce in Oma's backyard. I thought that was the tallest tree I had ever seen and wondered how airplanes could safely maneuver around it. We amused ourselves outdoors on the wooden gymnastic set with rings and bars built for adults. Catching bamboo rings with sticks after the rings had been tossed way up into the air was one of our favorite games. We used the second-floor kitchen balcony like a service elevator to lower and hoist buckets full of nonsense, pretending to help Annenie transport items to ground level. For the adults, preserving and canning fresh fruits and vegetables was an essential summer household task. My aunt Annenie labored diligently for days, making sure that enough produce was preserved to last the winter. Klaus and I loaded the tin cans of vegetables onto a little metal wagon and carefully pulled the load to the Verden cannery. After the tops were sealed, we hauled the load back to Oma's to be stored on shelves in the basement with the preserved fruits. Bushels of potatoes and apples lay heaped in the coldest, darkest corner of the basement to stay cool during the long winters and provide us with months of nutrition.

One of my favorite play areas was under the dining-room table. The tablecloth reached the floor, and it made a private world for me, with imaginary friends. The red velvet-covered dining chairs also had skirts to make my hideout more secluded. This "tent" was important. It provided security and comfort, and I pretended it was my own little house. My aunt and grandmother never interfered. Nor did they make me feel self-conscious about my desire for enjoying my "friends." They respected my space and called or knocked on the table before they entered my world.

Afternoons in Verden were set aside for our routine café klatch on the Aller River terrace, weather permitting. If we didn't already have pastries in the house, we strolled to the bakery and bought fresh strudel, tort, or meringues with whip cream—except we never had the cream. Each afternoon Klaus and I had to select our favorite china pattern for this occasion. We spent many concentrated moments in front of my grandmother's glass china cabinet scrutinizing the design and color of her many patterned porcelain dishes before making our final choice. This selection ritual was equally important to our food. Next, we loaded baskets and trays with china, linens, silver, cakes, hot chocolate, and coffee and carefully caravanned down the seven terraces to our garden sanctuary by the water. By today's standards, it was overkill on pomp and circumstance for just a bit of pastry, but it was worth it. The joy of relaxing in the scented, fresh air at the beautifully set table, overlooking the river scenes, meadows, and surrounding green paradise, temporarily superseded fear and thoughts of war. Impressionable events, even if momentary, turn the page in your memory bank. A child's nervous system heightened by fear, switches quickly between good and evil. Pleasure and beauty were such vital intermissions before the next siren.

Some days we merely walked along the river until we arrived at the Aller ferry house. A cable was stretched across the river and the ferry tender stood inside a small, wooden boat, like a fishing boat with seats built on each side, and pulled himself, boat, and passengers across by hand. There wasn't much on the other side except a never-ending meadow that stretched all the way to the horizon and a few cows. However, locals used the ferry and meadow crossing as a short cut to walk to other towns. Oma, Annenie, Klaus and I enjoyed the strolls amid the wildflowers and sometimes carried a fully loaded picnic basket along for our usual afternoon "tea" on the pasture. We befriended the ferry boat tender and his family and infrequently played with his children. My grandmother considered us of a different social class and discouraged us from fraternizing too often with the tender's offspring.

Klaus and I had our first swimming lessons in the Aller. There was a high pier near the ferry house and we took swimming lessons from one of the locals who lived on the river. We were harnessed around our chest and waist much like a dog harness with leather straps. The harness had a hook on the back of it and was connected to a strong line that was attached to a crane, similar to a huge fishing rod. We were reeled down over the side of the pier. When we hit the water we started flapping both arms and legs as if we were drowning. The coach shouted instructions to us, which we quickly put to use.

We discovered how to swim rather easily that way. We only learned the breast stroke.

Our summer vacations with Oma and Annenie were filled with lots of love, joy, and play. Vacations, typically, when school was in session, lasted no more than six weeks. Klaus and I exchanged frequent letters and cards on a regular basis with Mother. We did not make use of the telephone. I'm not sure why, unless many of the telephone lines were down due to bombings or the cost was too high. Verden was not one of the enemy's principal bombing targets. Cities with oil refineries, shipyards, railroads or other major industrial interests were considered strategic bomb sites. I don't believe we ever had air raids during our summers in Verden but we certainly were within sight and sound of bombs, cannons, fire, and smoke from terrorized cities. My aunt loved little children and had dreams of one day running her own orphanage. In later years she repeatedly expressed that the only really happy days she had were playing with Klaus and me. My grandmother was formal in her conduct, but also appreciated a good laugh and cheated whenever we played games. Some afternoons we enjoyed our routine café klatch at a favorite outdoor restaurant along the Aller River and took pleasure in the rippling patterns the mild summer breeze made on the flowers and grasses. I remember the tender branches from the Maple trees swaying overhead as we strolled along the sidewalk. We opened the seed pods and stuck them on our nose like a unicorn. The air smelled so sweet and wholesome. Especially on rainy days, the scent of boxwoods clung to our nostrils. It was heaven. War never crossed our mind. Strolling into the city of Verden was a special treat for Klaus and me. We always looked forward to that because the sidewalk led directly in front of the *Schweine Loch* (pig hole). This was one of our more memorable childhood events. Just a block before entering the town of Verden there was a farmer's home with a six foot high, painted green, wooden privacy fence blocking the barnyard from the sidewalk. There were grunting, smelling swine behind those old planks. The good news is that a knot had fallen out of one of the wooden planks. This hole, about two inches in diameter, was just exactly eye level for Klaus and me and we never, ever, passed by this *Schweine Loch* without peeping through the hole to inspect the pigs and inhale the familiar, primeval barnyard perfumes. (We returned to Germany in 1966 for our grandmother's ninetieth birthday and much to our surprise, nothing had changed and the *loch* was still there and so were the pigs. We know, because we couldn't pass without bending down and peeping through the hole once more). While on these walks, acquaintances nodded toward one another or acknowledged one another's existence, but it was considered improper to stop and hold a conversation in the middle of the street. Oma, dressed in navy blue or black, kept an eye out for those older ladies who dared to put on youthful, bright apparel. Oma was decidedly class conscious and considered such people of the bourgeois or lower class. She interfaced with commoners only for business and necessity. My aunt, on the other hand, was not nearly as formal. She belonged to a group similar to the Red Cross and believed in being charitable and helpful. Once, while we were walking through town, Annenie saw a sick child and tenderly helped the little boy back to his home. Mother said that Annenie was a beautiful young lady and had many suitors, but Oma criticized all of them and thought none were good enough for her daughter. Consequently, Annenie never married.

Summers were especially enjoyable when our Onkel Wolfgang and his wife Gerda visited in Verden. Onkel Wolfgang was a music teacher in Hanover, Germany. He and his wife were among Mother's favorite relatives. Wolfgang was forever humming, singing or playing the piano or cracking jokes. If the weather was nice, Annenie would make a picnic lunch for us and we'd take the train into the countryside. We stepped off at some small "Dorf" and hiked into the hills along wooded trails and over meadows, while Uncle Wolfgang wandered ahead of us wildly flinging his arms into the air, conducting us in song as we followed him like the Pied Piper. All the Ritters had good singing voices. If anyone was lost we used the Ritter whistle to meet up again. There was one tune for calling and another tune for answering. This has always been our standard way of communicating in a crowd when we lost sight of each other. Evenings at Oma's were game time. We played card games and rolled dice. As Klaus and I later learned, all the adults cheated to inflict the "Schlafmütze" (sleeping cap) status on us. I don't recall the rules of the game, but someone asks a question and if the answer doesn't come quickly enough, the other players lay their cards down and the loser puts a sleeping cap on his head. These were routine summer days in Verden.

CALL   RESPONSE

Ritter Whistle

Summers at Frankfurt and the Baltic

On one rare occasion Mother sent us to summer camp at Frankfurt am Main, which is, as the name implies, on the Main River in southwestern Germany. Among English speakers it is usually known as simply Frankfurt, but Germans call it by its full name so as to distinguish it from another Frankfurt in Germany, Frankfurt an der Oder. In the Holy Roman Empire, Frankfurt was one of the most important cities where German kings and emperors were elected since 855. It was the revolutionary capital and the seat of the first democratically elected German parliament. Frankfurt hoped to be the new capital city of Germany after World War II. However, Konrad Adenauer (the first post-World War II chancellor) preferred the tiny city of Bonn, for the most part because it was his hometown, but also the Germans feared that making Frankfurt the capital of West Germany would give the Americans too much influence over the German government, as Frankfurt was the headquarters-city of the United States zone of the Allied occupation

Camp in Frankfurt was an experience but not necessarily all good. I didn't enjoy being that far from family or familiar adults. It was a large, plush camp, with buildings several stories high. Each floor had one long balcony running the length of the building. We had a definite routine early each morning, beginning with vigorous exercises on the balcony and cold showers afterward. Like any camp, we took field trips. One such trip was fifty miles northwest of our camp to the Neuhof-Ellers salt mine. We saw what impressed us as skyscraper salt licks in the city. We never went down into the mine. Girls and boys were always separated, and I didn't get to see much of Klaus. On one of our hikes, our group of girls heard hollering behind the bushes, and as we sneaked close to the noise, we saw a group of young boys taking turns swatting their belts across the buttocks of a kid who was leaning over a log. This punishment was definitely supervised. The boy had stolen something from the dormitory, and each boy in the dorm was instructed to give the offender one swat on the behind. I'm guessing the embarrassment was worse than the belts. While at camp, Klaus had to be quarantined with the mumps. When we arrived home, Mother had just gotten over her own case of the mumps, which she had at exactly the same time as Klaus's. The doctor figured she had either contracted the mumps from one of the letters he wrote home while ill, or she had sympathy symptoms. We were rarely seriously ill but I do remember that when all three of us had fish poison we had to take large, black charcoal tablets to settle our convulsions. On another occasion nurses at the hospital fed me oatmeal water, spoon by spoon, for an upset stomach. For the most part we decided the cures were worse than our illnesses.

Mother also took us to the beach on occasion. The place I remember most is Seebad Heringsdorf. It is a tourist town located northwest of Hamburg on the Baltic Sea. Heringsdorf, once a small fishing village, became a seaside resort on the north coast of the Usedom Island. The village has beautiful flora and is surrounded by white beaches. The climate tends to be more temperate than in central Germany. It is considered one of the most popular seaside resorts on the German Baltic shore. The houses in Heringsdorf are built in the classical style during the reign of Kaiser Wilhelm II—late 1800s to early 1900s. In particular, I remember the whiteness of the sand and the hooded wicker seats scattered along the shore that provide protection from the sun. Two adults could easily sit in one chair. Also, it was popular to have a man dressed in a polar-bear suit visit the children on the beach. Mother had a picture taken of all three of us with the "bear."

Our grandparents home in Verden an der Aller

Oma, Onkel Wolfgang, and I on the
Verden house entrance tile walk.

Klaus and I pouring hot chocolate on Oma's Aller River alcove

Mother, Klaus and I at Seebad Heringsdorf beach

Tante Annenie

FRIENDS

*I doubt whether anything in the world can beautify a soul
more readily, more naturally, than the knowledge that
somewhere in its neighborhood there exists a pure and
noble friend whom it can trust and love.* A. E. Ritter, *Murmurings.* p. 1

MOTHER HAD MANY personal friends in Germany who were
more like family to her. In Germany, she made friends easily and,
despite her American citizenship and strong foreign accent, had
multitudes of engaging companions from different genders and
backgrounds. The cast included all categories of characters. Mother
had always had a flair for interesting and often eccentric folks. Some
were religious, some were party people, homosexuals, wild women,
professors, Jews, Christians, agnostics, young, and old, etc. Whatever
their mindset, they all had an intellectual flair and were fascinating.
It was Mother's nature to treat each person exactly the same, with
sincerity, dignity, and respect. She sought the good in people and
capitalized on their positive characteristics. I've always appreciated
that about Mother.

As the war escalated and schools were closed for longer and longer
periods of time, Klaus and I had many days that stretched into weeks
and months without school. During these times, Mother took us into
the country where she hoped we would be out of harm's way. Making
the acquaintance and nurturing our relationships with farm families
in neighboring rural communities probably saved our life. Frequently,
she left us with the Unteutsches for the work week while she returned
to Hamburg. We became especially close to two families. The

Unteutsch and Mickel-Garbers families in the Lüneburger Heide became our home away from the city. These farmers were exceptional in their kindness and generosity, and we effortlessly merged into their culture and lifestyle, not only out of necessity but also out of love. The Unteutsch family lived in Jesteburg, which was less than fifty miles south of Hamburg and easily accessible by commuter train. They were like relatives to us, and Klaus and I called them aunt and uncle. Their house was a good forty-five-minute walk from the Jesteburg train station—mostly on unpaved roads winding through grain fields. Erhard and Martha Unteutsch and their six children— Erhard, Johannes, Erika, Georg, Reinhard, and Waltraud—lived on the farm. The children were older than Klaus and I. The youngest was just a year or two older than we. The oldest two boys were in the military. Uncle Erhard was employed near Hamburg in a tea firm and took the train to work each day. Tante Martha was a devout Christian, and Mother called her as close to an angel as was humanly possible. Georg, in his late teens, was exempt from military duty and permitted by the German government to remain on the farm and help his parents. He and Tante Martha ran the farm with war-prisoner help—mostly Polish and Italian. To supplement their income, they also rented small primitive cottages in the woods to city visitors. Each cottage had its own name. Our favorite cottage was called the Piltz (mushroom). The Piltz was completely round with bunk beds lining the inside wall. The bunks also served as benches when a table was pulled up. The center was living space. The thatched roof extended way beyond the round walls, which gave it the appearance of a mushroom. All the cottages were private and out of common view. Guests took their meals at the farmhouse. On special occasions, when the cottages weren't rented, all of us kids were allowed to spend the night together, alone in one of the cottages. We played and told stories until near dawn when we finally collapsed into bed in unison. Mother became dependent on the Unteutsches for our retreat away from the city.

The farmhouse was typical of most European farms where the living quarters are connected to the cow or pig stables by a covered walkway or a barn. At the Unteutsch farm, the galley kitchen adjoined the barn. The barn was large enough for five cow stalls, several pigs, and a hay loft above. It was connected to the house by a covered drive-through for heavy farm machinery—which was abandoned in the back yard due to fuel shortage. It also had a separate room off to the side for servants. Their house was a two-story brick house with a walk-in foyer, living/dining room to the left, two bedrooms at the end and the kitchen eating area to the right, joining the galley. Upstairs were more bedrooms and a smoke closet where meat and fish were cured. As standard for many farms, in front of the house was a large barnyard with chickens and ducks, plus a peacock or two, and rabbit cages near the stables. In the back was the vegetable and flower garden. The house sat back off the unpaved road about three hundred feet into the woods. Farm fields were beyond the woods. Besides Georg, the other children were in school and too young for military service or farming. Major crops on the Unteutsch farm were potatoes, asparagus, green peas, snap peas, string beans, carrots, and cabbage. They also grew strawberries and blueberries in summer and the woods were full of wild blueberries, blackberries, and mushrooms. Frequently we packed lunch and piled onto the gelding drawn wagon to spend a full day in the forest picking berries. For supper we looked forward to eating bowlfuls of berries with milk and sugar. Harvesting berries, like searching for mushrooms, was part of survival. Klaus and I had to milk cows and go on mushroom forays just like all the other kids. Whatever we brought home is what we ate. We had our fill of sautéed mushrooms. We enjoyed stalking through the forest and rooting under trees with sticks, and became quite skilled at identifying mushroom varieties. Berries and mushrooms were not the only surprises in the woods. Deep in the forest, hidden among thick, plush conifers, and covered up with burlap, twigs and leaves we discovered a car. We reported this find to the adults who explained to us its significance and impressed upon us the consequence if we ever told anyone. It appears that one of Mother's friends owned the car and didn't want it confiscated so he asked the Unteutsches if he could hide it in their woods. It was a beautiful, deep maroon Mercedes-Benz. Special permission was required from the government to own an automobile or any petroleum-consuming vehicle. Petrol was only used for military vehicles or necessary commerce. Even farm equipment sat idle without fuel. Commercial production for nonmilitary equipment was suspended, and all private automobiles were confiscated and converted to military or government use. I loved this car. The inside was real leather, also maroon and smelled rich. I always thought that when I grew up I would own a car like that. We checked on the car periodically as we roamed and played in the woods, but we kept our word and made sure we weren't followed whenever we went back to admire and dream over our discovery.

A balanced diet was not easy to maintain during the war and nearly every purchase required a ration card. My aunt and Mother only smoked at parties—maybe one pack a year. Pall Mall was Annenie's favorite brand of cigarette. However, the cigarette cards made good legal tender and Mother was always able to swap her cigarette cards for sugar cards with some addict eager to make a trade. Fresh vegetables and dairy products were scarce in the city. The farm supplemented our diets. Chickens were raised mostly for eggs and were butchered only for special feasts. Rabbit meat provided a main source of protein. Chickens on our friend's farm were fed pulverized porcelain that we ground ourselves from broken dishes and crushed eggshells for their calcium intake. In order to keep the hens as productive egg layers, Tante Martha took the eggs from the chickens' nests, wrapped them in a towel, and put them in bed with her at night to keep them warm until they were ready to hatch. I'm not sure how she kept them warm during the day. Just before hatching, she returned each egg to the nest and the hens happily sat on the eggs and seemed delighted that someone else incubated their chicks. Frankly, I always thought it would be a mighty gooey mess if any of the eggs ever broke in bed. But the system worked and no eggs ever broke in bed. We loved the farm and the family. Across the dirt road was a lake stocked with fish and eels. We walked the goat to greener pastures, fished and swam (sometimes in the nude) and dug clay out of the hillside to make miniature sun-baked pottery. We also played hide and seek in treetops and rode clumsy field horses to and from the potato fields. As I discovered by standing too close to the hindquarters of one of the huge Clydesdale-type horses, their kick can raise you off your feet and leave a horseshoe tattoo on your thigh that lasts about as long as the exaggerated jokes and embarrassment.

Foreign prisoners supplemented farm help because all the able-bodied German men were fighting on the front. The Unteutsches had one Italian male prisoner and a Polish mother with a new-born baby. The young Italian man was tremendously entertaining and in the evenings he taught us new swift-footed jump rope tricks and impressed us with his fancy jumping skills. He spoke little German. The young Polish mother and her young, new-born baby occupied the servant's room off the barn. She spoke no German, was quite plump and homely, but a sweet mother. We loved to visit her at mealtime. We watched her wean the infant by chewing up solid food and spitting the pureed victuals on a spoon to feed to the baby. Another "permanent" occupant on the farm was an elderly mother with her quadriplegic son. He appeared to be in his early twenties and was totally paralyzed. The mother had to feed and bathe him. Whenever the sun shone she rolled him into the back garden in a reclining wheelchair. We didn't pay much attention to the two. They occupied one of the downstairs bedrooms. I think the mother did a few menial chores in the garden and cleaned vegetables to pay for her stay. Mostly, I believe, Tante Martha took pity on the two. Her husband had been killed in the war. On one of our return visits to the Unteutsch farm we noticed the old woman without her son. She looked weak and utterly despondent Tante Martha told us that her son became ill and never returned from the hospital. Later we overheard the adults say that doctors told the mother that her son had choked on porridge while at the hospital and died. But we all knew that this was no accident. Basically, he was an unproductive consumer during hard times. I believe the mother grieved herself to death. Another regular at the Unteutsch farm was Herr Schwartz. Herr Schwartz was probably in his late sixties, partially bald, short, and round. He was an eccentric bachelor who had the peculiar habit of pureeing the food in his mouth before swallowing. Whenever he drank coffee or slurped soup or anything that was remotely liquid, he sloshed it through his teeth back and forth, several times, before swallowing. Our evening meal usually consisted of clabber sprinkled with a bit of sugar, bread, butter, and cold leftovers. Herr Schwartz put the clabber into his mouth and his cheeks puffed out as he began the liquefying process. It sounded like he was rinsing his mouth out after brushing his teeth. All the kids at the table smirked and cocked eyes at one another. He was so totally self-absorbed that it was obvious our stares and twinkling eyes had no affect on him.

Tante Martha was the only clairvoyant person whom I have ever known. She saw her son get killed by an explosive force while in combat. She described it to us in detail. On one of our visits, Mother, Klaus, and I were sleeping upstairs over the master bedroom where Tante Martha and Onkel Erhard slept. All three of us were awakened by such a scream coming from below that we were momentarily paralyzed with fear. The three of us scrambled down the stairs in our nightclothes to find Tante Martha hysterically crying in bed and Onkel Erhard comforting her. Onkel Erhard tried to convince Martha that she had had a nightmare and it was just a dream. After she reconciled herself to what she knew to be the truth, she said in a soft and calm voice, "No, I saw it. Johannes is dead." Erhard insisted it was a dream. But she was persistent and sure of her vision. She explained how she clearly saw Johannes's face at the instant of death. Tante Martha described in expressionless detail and vivid color how the event unfolded before her mind's eyes. She said, "Johannes's body was flung up from a trench, his arms were thrown up above his head, and there was blood splattered across his face—as if reacting to a mine or grenade explosion." Even as a young child, I could "see" exactly what she was describing. I still can. She was calm, as she has always been, yet teary. She knew he was with God. We were all in a state of shock. No one said anything. It was too real not to believe her, yet who had ever witnessed such as this. We tried to sleep through the rest of the night. The next morning, as usual, Onkel Erhard took the train to Hamburg to his job at the tea factory. Tante Martha was quiet but went about her normal chores. That evening, we kids were playing in the courtyard when we saw Onkel Erhard returning from work, walking through the woods toward us. We observed that he had been crying. His eyes were painfully red. We saw a white piece of paper sticking out of the left breast pocket of his dark coat jacket. It was a telegram from the German War Department, telling him that their son was killed on the battlefield in the line of duty. As he came within close range, he reached for the telegram and held it out to his wife. Tante Martha walked toward her husband to greet and comfort him. She said, "I know, I know. Johannes is with God. It will be all right."

The Mickel-Garbers family was equally important to our survival during the war years. They also lived south of Hamburg in the heather country. Mother met them through the Unteutsches. They lived in a town called Marxen. Marxen, Kreis Harburg, was within a long day's walk of Jesteburg. If one hiked across pastures and climbed over fences in a direct line as the crow flies—which we often did—we could reach Marxen, where Georg and Herta lived, by sundown. They had three young adult children: Erica, Inge, and Jürgen. Since Herta Garbers was the last Garbers in her family, they combined their names when she married Georg Mickel. Georg Mickel-Garbers was a member of the Nazi Party and Mother's only Nazi friend. He was tall, robust, nice looking, with a head full of curly white hair. Herta was a kind, dependable, hardworking wife and mother. Her appearance was homely but neat. Her gray hair was pulled back into a tightly twisted bun at the back of her neck, and her dress was plain. She was a pedantic housekeeper, and no mud from the farm lay on the floor long enough to dry. Onkel Georg became quite fond of Mother who was vivacious, good-looking, highly regarded, and interesting. The opportunities for romance and passion were tempting. Herta was honest and direct in her relationship with Mother, and they held a deep mutual respect for each other. She was not blind to the attraction between Mother and her husband and openly confronted Mother and begged her not to take her husband away. Herta need not have asked Mother to control her desire since Mother's focus remained on her two children's survival, and any deviation from that goal was nonnegotiable. There were no exceptions. Tante Herta and Onkel Georg remained our trustworthy friends until their death. Like the Unteutsch family, the Mickel-Garbers were among our closest and best friends, and we also called them aunt and uncle. Georg Mickel-Garbers was financially secure and owned much land, in part due to his connection with the Nazi Party. Though not ostentatious or elegant, their house was interesting and comfortable and plenty big for family and friends. He had at least half a dozen horses, several herds of cattle, and lots of pigs, plus a couple of large dogs. The two-story brick house was connected to a covered walkway leading to the pig stalls. The piazzalike barnyard was enormous to us children in comparison to most farm homes. It appeared to be the dimensions of an unpaved square the size of a parade ground. An adult-high red brick wall shielded the farm from the road. The family home was to the left of the farm yard as one entered the tractor-wide gate. Straight back from the piazza was a large hay and grain barn, and directly across from the home, to the right of the entrance, were the cattle and horse stables. Behind the stables were several smaller servant homes and two tall silos. Pastures and wheat fields lay behind the barns. The vegetable, fruit, flower, and berry garden was again in the back of the house behind the kitchen. The Mickel-Garbers had a spacious covered porch on the side of their house with steps leading to a manicured lawn outlined with flowers. I particularly loved their entrance hall. Just as you came in the front door, to the right under the staircase, there hung a long light chestnut-brown horse's tail. The horsehair was shiny and well-groomed. It nearly reached the floor. It was considered good luck to hang a horse's tail in the foyer. We frequently stayed with the Mickel-Garbers when air raids were forecast for the cities. These forecasts were like weather reports: not dependable but not to be ignored. Sometimes when we had no school in Hamburg, we attended the one-room country school in Marxen. No one cared if visiting children just walked in and took lessons with the regulars. The first graders sat in the front row, and the upper grades sat in the back—much like country schools in America.

I have particularly good memories of our after-supper entertainment with the Mickel-Garbers family. It was anticipated in many European homes to remain at the table after the evening meal. While the women cleared the table, men reached for their nearby musical instruments such as a violin, guitar, accordion, or harmonica. First, conversation started with stories, the day's events, politics, and jokes; then someone began a favorite tune, and before long, children and adults were singing and often dancing. Despite the dangers of war, these enchanting interludes were among our happiest moments. *Gemütlich* is what the Germans say of a cozy evening with loved ones.

Martha and Erhard Unteutsch

Erhard and Martha Unteutsch with their son,
Johannes, who was killed in the war.

Mother with Tante Martha 1946.

Herta and Georg Mickel-Garbers;

Mickel-Garbers farm

WAY OF LIFE

*Work, work—hard and the discipline it involves has
an indelible mark on the character. It charges batteries
and offers a direction for confused bewildered lives.*
A. E. Ritter, *Murmurings.* p. 144

IN HAMBURG, MOTHER continued her duties at the consulate
as regularly as she could, depending on conditions of war. At this
time, Klaus and I were not yet of school age, but we attended
kindergarten. Kindergarten was unpleasant. My recollection was that
it was dark and dull. I spent most of my time waiting for Mother to
pick me up. Kindergarten provided me with head lice, little else. My
thick long braids were an easy target. However, lice were the reason
for cozy evenings sitting on the floor in front of the divan while Mother
and Klaus gave me their undivided attention even if it was just picking
little parasites out of my hair by hand and combing my hair with a
louse comb. The fact that all our coats and caps hung crowded on
the cloak rack spread the pests quickly to the entire class. Lice were
dreaded by all the schools and considered a major problem by
German health officials.

I read in some of Mother's letters that we were stinging cold. I
guess I was never warm in winter, so I really don't remember
complaining about the cold. I do remember that we always wore
heavy under and outer garments and that bathing was a frigid,
frightful, and much-dreaded experience. Young girls wore long
densely woven, cotton sweatpants under their skirts or dresses. Slacks
were unknown, and ladies wore thick natural-colored cotton stockings

to keep their legs warm. Mother had several fur coats and collars. I also owned a fur muff that hung around my neck by a string so I wouldn't drop it. I thought it to be the most wonderful feeling to reach my hands into the soft tunnel of the muff. We used hot water bottles or warmed bricks wrapped in a towel in bed to get us started on the thawing process at night, and we frequently dressed in the mornings under the covers. Our breakfast was nearly always oatmeal or farina with butter or just plain—never sugar and cream. Our diet consisted basically of irish potatoes, cabbage, rutabagas, and black bread. Early in the war years, we had access to other foods, but they were not plentiful and were rather expensive. Dairy products were at a premium, and we learned to eat and enjoy schmaltz on our thick black bread instead of butter. We never went hungry, and I accepted and even liked most foods, except the popular wartime staple: beets. My favorite meals were sliced pan-fried potatoes and vanilla soup with whipped egg-white dollops on top. Neither Klaus nor I cared for meat. Mother was a confirmed carnivore and suffered from the lack of ham or any part of a pig and good Southern soul food—turnip greens, sweet potatoes, and corn bread—totally unheard of in Germany. She never made an issue of hardships, and we accepted our diet the way we accepted the cold and the bombings. Our stomachs and hearts were satisfied, and soliciting pity for want of pleasure was unacceptable. Klaus and I heard little of politics on the radio. Mother believed in strict censorship for her children, and at all times, we were spared any news that "might corrupt our delicate and innocent minds," as she often said.

Below are two more letters Mother wrote in 1940. The first one is correspondence with Emily Frojen written in July. Mother wrote the second letter to her sister Annie Lee Fenn, in Clayton, Alabama.

July 19, 1940

Emily, my dear!

Just a few words to say that "all is well" with the Ritters which message, I hope, will still find your generous heart interested. I think so often of you and the children and I'm constantly wondering when and how your little family will all get back together. Is Mr. Frojen still in Norway? I have wondered why he doesn't show up at the Consulate anymore. Could it be that he has already joined you in the States?

Much has happened the past year since your departure from Hamburg. An estimate of perhaps 500 have been killed by the English attacks or injured. About 150 dead and the others either seriously or slightly injured. Last Sunday evening I was rather sure that my time had arrived too. Bombs fell rather generously within 2 blocks of us and the fighting took place directly overhead. I observed it for quite some time with a sadistic interest, common to the custom in Germany. The schools were suddenly closed about two weeks ago and children were advised to leave the city. I permitted Herr Hauptman Ritter to take Klaus and Katharine to the Grossmutter in Verden/Aller. It isn't safe there either but no siren disturbs them in the night and they are able to sleep through without having to hear the worst. They will return to Hamburg on August the second and on the third we shall all three leave the early train for Heringsdorf on the Ostsee (Baltic). For the first time in years and years, my dear, I am going to have a real vacation. I shall return to the Consulate toward the end of August, at which time I hope the war will have passed into history and the Frojen family will be on their way toward their Hamburg home. This is to say, of course, if the Consulate still exists. We have literally nothing to do except to twiddle the thumbs all day and the U.S. government cannot get rich like that. We anticipate a daily cut in the staff. Shall I begin all over again? I dare not dream of fame in this world for just so sure am I riding for a fall, but come as it may; "die Welt ist schön." Nicht wahr, Mein Süßes? (The world is beautiful. Isn't that so my sweets?)

By the time my letter reaches you I predict either that peace will already be in the air or a most terrible war will have begun on both sides of us. Just today we are all pitched with nerves awaiting the Reichstag meeting tonight at 7:O'clock. Either peace plans with England or war against Russia seems predictable. What will America do? My heart still carries back to the land of my beginning, and both consciously and otherwise I catch myself defending her. In other words I'm becoming a Nationalistic American citizen on the wrong side of the ocean. Will Roosevelt win out or be brought in as President again? Do you want him again? I'm so eager to hear all that you have to say about world affairs now and if your appreciation of Germany has gone up or down during these months of absence.

Is Marie happy in the American schools? Some months ago the Monckebergs came by for an evening. Armadeus is in the H. University now and looks rather lovable but they are all so fanatic and one-sided in this fight that I felt tremendously relieved when they had departed. I have let the friendship gradually suffocate. Armadeus would be adorable with any other mother in the world but his real one is a "Pulverfast." Poor Marie would have to put a pill in her coffee before considering the son. I'm inclined to think that they still have their eyes on her though. (Your little girl—get what I mean)

July 24, 1940

Well, here I am again after a weeks pause. In the meantime we spend each evening a couple of hours in the cellar listening to the bombing and fighting between the Heinies & Tommies. The latter are still holding out entirely alone and are putting up a brave fight although no definite plan for fighting seems to have been arranged. In other words the English appear to have gone into this fight without proper preparations. I don't understand it. I know that they figured that America would come to their rescue but even at that they have thoroughly disappointed their friends throughout the world. And what will be the outcome? At present it appears that Germany will have "bagged the works" in another months time unless something unforeseen develops. The thing that interests me most just now is to have it all over. My already tangled nerves haven't improved a bit under the load. Living conditions, as you probably can imagine, are controlled to the utmost, and instead of personal friendship and love increasing under the ever constant danger of death, it has more than ever definitely "gone with the wind." Suspicion, jealousy, and hate are all riding high. Not a pretty picture to paint to you of your future home but you understand so beautifully how to take things with a dose of salts.

I am all agog to see you again, and perhaps I, too, shall know what it means to be jealous then. With that girlhood "figger" of yours and the charm of California peace I can well imagine that you have turned back the years in uncertain numbers. I on the other hand am growing gray by leaps and bounds and I'm still hesitating about cutting the braids. I think I'm waiting for you to return and give me a push. I want it off but I fear the worst. I have known a few stout people that looked just impossible with short hair and a number of slim ones here in the Consulate also appear like Polish servants. So what?

We have a new man-Consul Woodford—with us now. I like him too which opinion goes to say that I consider him to be a MAN. He is short both in statue and in words, is married, is originally from Kentucky but his wife is now in Chicago. Mr. Keblinger is still here and still madly in love with his secretary. O, these secretaries, my dear! What a life of Riley they lead. If you want Marie to feather her nest just let her be a private secretary, and I'm not so sure I wouldn't have her be. At least a girl has a chance of first fiddle in this way.

The weather has been worse than rotten all summer. We froze all winter and have so far known the coldest and darkest summer ever in Hamburg. One must put up a good fight to keep the sprits high. I am hoping that August will prove better and that the children and I shall have a chance to thaw up on the Baltic.

Hurry back to your pretty little home here and don't forget us. Remember it is possible to miss a friend more than a lover in the things that matter most to the inward being.

Love to each of you,
Aurora & children—

I wanted to send your letter by air-mail but the P.O. tells me that America has discontinued it. I shall therefore ask permission to use the pouch that goes out this evening.

Italy also has closed all borders so that the Jews from Germany are now compelled to go across Russia and Japan to reach the States, and even if we are compelled to get out, I do not know how it could be accomplished. I hope anyway that it doesn't come that far. Of course, the Consulate is nervous—

Mr. Chase has been transferred to Berne, Switzerland, and Mr. Thayer to Moscow. Mr. Abbott is here in the same home with the same maid, but Mrs. A. is in Washington. Mrs. Dalferes and son are in southern France and Mr. Dalferes is alone in the apartment. Mr. and Mrs. Magnumson are quite the same. Mr. Keblinger has already announced his intentions of resigning at the end of the year and being pensioned. We surmise that he will marry his secretary, Miss Otten, and perhaps take her with him back to the States. She is German and no Foreign Service Officer is now allowed to marry a foreigner while in active duty; hence perhaps the resignation. Miss Otten is in her middle 30ties and he in the middle 60ties. Don't' repeat this in letters back here. It is only Consulate "Klatsch."

Just like you to ask if you can do something for us. No, thanks, my dear. You have done too much already. We are all comfortably clothed and are even getting fat on the war food. All that we need at the moment is PEACE and plenty of it, but you can't turn that trick for us at so great a distance. We have no fresh fruits whatsoever and few vegetables but one can still satisfy his appetite with the various substitutes on the market.

I went by your home the other day and as usual the blinds are drawn. I judge that Mr. Frojen gave all orders on his last trip here. He came into the Consulate shortly before the fall of Norway and the subsequent bombing of Oslo. I've thought so much of him since that time. Did he come through safely? I have heard nothing to the contrary here in the office. The pouch is being closed to be sent to Berlin so I'll hurry this off. Am relieving at the telephone as one of the staff has vacation now. I'll be glad to get back in my shipping department when it's all over.

Love to each and to the children, and soon I shall hope to see you gain in Hamburg.

Aurora

November 20, 1940

My Dearest Annie and family,

Although I wrote to you last week, I shall hurriedly add a few words more only to say that up to date we are all well and that we think daily in great anticipation of our American home, and the possibility of some day seeing it again. Last week we experienced some frantic and most destructive air-battles. On Friday night the first sirens notified us at 8: in the P.M. that English bombers were overhead—some 40 or more. Immediately thereafter the whole sky was alight with the thousand and one search lights used to blind the pilots and prevent them from successfully hitting the desired point. Then the German chasing planes started out after the enemy planes, then the raining of bombs, and the thundering of untold cannons. This continued throughout the entire night, sometimes paralyzing us with uncertainty as to our fate, then ceasing for a moment only to return again more destructive than ever. The final warning came at 5:30 in the A.M. and we were able with some amount of certainty to return to our unused beds—only to rise again for the office one hour later. One learns somehow to live without sleep and to be normally reserved and fatalistic as to their fortune or misfortune. Strange as it may seem too, one feels an almost unbelievable calm in the midst of the battle—a kind of watching and waiting feeling for death to claim its own. All fear is lost when the fighting is directly overhead and when you realize that immediate neighbors have been one of the unfortunates. I packed Klaus and Katharine closely together in the safest spot possible deep in the cellar of our home—and then I bent over them and held their hands while they sleepily dozed in half-consciousness as to the seriousness of the consequences of the night. Some 1100 bombs were thrown on Hamburg on Friday between evening and dawn, and Saturday night was perhaps even worse and somewhat longer in duration. Since then however, we have enjoyed a couple of hours of undisturbed sleep and the war now seems only a sad impossible sort of a dream. That's the way life runs here now; a division marked by dreadful realism or a happy idealism. Death seems to be everywhere, and if you aren't one of the dead, you are mighty glad to laugh and be happy and live a full day. None of us can escape the inevitable and I'm not so sure if it matters tremendously just when the hour overtakes us. I have not the slightest fear of death but I do so dislike the thought that I could be maimed or helpless for life. *Well, perhaps neither shall happen!*

I have a feeling that we shall be among the living left to tell the tale and on this I concentrate. I like to feel that way, and I worry comparatively little. You also may rest calmly over winter with a certain confidence about us. I anticipate that the winter months will be quiet ones because of the dark nights and the rainy, windy weather. Perhaps the spring will again be more serious but that's many days and weeks in the future. Even an unanticipated peace could take place before then. So again, my dear, DON'T WORRY—Just believe that we'll live to eat you out of your house and home some sweet day, and you'll probably find that it comes true.

Will William come home for Christmas? Is he doing well? Tell me about the other boys too. Is Will's asthma better? Have him try a nice steaming fresh hot cup of coffee when he feels an attack coming on and perhaps it will give him remarkable relief. I have a friend here with heart-asthma and that is her most comforting remedy. I would make it fresh and strong though—either with milk and sugar or without.

Love and kisses from the three of us
Aurora and cubs

P.S. Soon You'll have another birthday and another Christmas too, eh? Well, make it a happy one and appreciate that you really are happy. With flowers, birds, and sunshine at your door, don't' worry about the troubles yet unborn. Keep the chin up even if it is getting a bit double with years.

TRAPPED

But, we can't always do what we want to do.
Rituals of fear sedate us all. Man is never free.
A. E. Ritter, *Murmurings*, p. 198

THE AMERICAN CONSULATE in Hamburg was scheduled for closure by July 8, 1941. A news flash in Hamburg published by Lloyd Lehrbas, an Associated Press staff writer, reads:

> EXPELLED U.S. CONSULS HEAD FOR PORTUGAL; WILL SAIL FRIDAY. More than 300 To Leave Lisbon Aboard Navy Transport West Point. More than 300 American consular officials and employees and their families—ordered out of Axis-dominated Europe when Axis officials were expelled from the United States moved today toward Lisbon, Portugal, from where they will sail for New York on Friday aboard the Navy transport WEST POINT. (ref. 10, p. 178)

Mother, Klaus, and I were among the three hundred ordered out of Germany. The dictate for Americans to flee Germany and return to the United States put a heavy burden on Mother. She was happy at the prospect of being reunited with her family, but concerned that the German government considered Klaus and me German citizens. She decided to take the risk and proceeded with plans for our move. Upon notice of the forthcoming closure of the consulate, Mother sold and gave away furniture and all nonessential items, and basically reduced our holdings to clothes, jewelry, baby scrapbooks, documents and artwork. Since Germany had closed almost all of its harbors and borders to anyone escaping the country, the three of us were booked by rail to Lisbon for passage to New York on the navy transport *West Point*. It would take us several days by train to travel over sixteen hundred miles through France and Spain before we reached Portugal. The first leg of our journey was to Frankfurt, Germany. We had a hotel room reserved for us in Frankfurt for one night and then were scheduled to continue the next day to cross the German border into France. The following morning, as we were getting ready to leave the hotel, Klaus and I sensed that something was seriously wrong. Mother was unaccustomedly restless and nervous. She didn't want to talk. Her facial expression was serious and strained as she paced the floor in our room. Klaus and I were worried and kept our eyes focused on our Mother. I remember asking her if something was wrong. She gave a cryptic answer. Suddenly, we heard a knock on our hotel room door. When Mother opened the door, two men dressed in dark business suits, stepped into the room and asked her to come with them to the German foreign service bureau. They said it was necessary for her to sign a few forms before we continued our journey. They assured Mother that this was strictly routine and that the procedure would be expedited if she left Klaus and me in the hotel while she took care of business. One of the men, they said, would stay with us until she returned. Mother's voice was frightened but unyielding as she told the men she was not going anywhere without her children. After some debating, they agreed for Klaus and me to come along.

It was a short drive into the heart of Frankfurt before we stopped in front of a multi-story government building where we were told to get out of the car. The two men escorted us up two flights of steps to the second floor and into the first door on the right of the hall. The office space we entered into was a corner room of classroom-size proportions, with windows across the back and left side. The room was lighted and the atmosphere civil and quiet. There appeared to be about thirty workstations behind the chest-high service counter that ran the full length of the office. Suspiciously the office was empty, except for three or four employees on duty that day, otherwise the environment seemed copasetic. A pleasant lady in her mid-forties with a sullen expression, wearing a dull outfit, stepped forward from behind the counter and directed us to have a seat in an open waiting area against the wall. The waiting zone was built like a jury box with bulky arm chairs arranged in two evenly spaced rows behind a heavy wooden railing. We sat and waited. After a few minutes a tall, lean gentleman clad in professional attire entered from the hall and greeted us cordially. He asked Mother to step into his office for a few minutes to sign necessary documentation before we could continue our journey. After some altercations, he finally convinced Mother that this was strictly routine and Klaus and I could sit right where we were and she'd be out in a minute. He led her into the corridor and around the corner out of our view. Hardly had the sound of Mother's footsteps faded when my father's brother, Hans, whom we barely knew, grabbed Klaus and me by our hands and coaxed and pulled us down the steps and toward the street exit. Totally confused, we hesitatingly resisted. We knew he was family, but we also knew something evil was taking place. As we were hustled toward the exit, I remember glancing over my shoulder toward the frosted glass door at the end of the hall. I knew with certainty Mother was behind that door. Struggling, Hans scuttled us into the street. Klaus snatched his hand away from Hans and ran back into the building and hid behind one of the massive wood and brass entrance doors. He was seized by one of the familiar male faces who was herding us toward the exit and preventing us from racing back upstairs. He grabbed Klaus and returned him to the grasp of Hans who pulled us to the train station. There was no waiting on the station platform as we immediately boarded the train for an unknown destination. Apparently this abduction had been in the planning stage for some time. The schedule clicked to precision. Klaus and I were dazed and refused to speak to Hans except to ask about our mother. I hugged the window side of the bench and fixed my gaze at the gray scenery as it reeled by. Onkel Hans tried to reassure us that it was for our best interest, but we just wanted to know where Mother was. He kept repeating that she was fine and was continuing on to America. By early afternoon the train stopped about forty miles northwest of Hamburg, in a small town called Ratzeburg. Ratzeburg is a quaint, historic city with a thousand-year-old history. In 1941, during our confinement, the population was between five and six thousand. Hans delivered us to a small, private home on a street where all the two-story, red brick houses looked completely alike with high-pitched, gabled roofs with dormers. My mental picture reminds me of a child's drawing with pointed houses and lollypop trees placed symmetrically along each side of the street. The picture was boring and sterile. The home we entered was on the right side of the street as we approached. The inside was plain, antiseptic, and sparsely furnished with angular utilitarian furniture. The floors were wood and sheer curtains hung on each window. Nothing was color-coordinated or decorated. The entire house gave the appearance of a hotel room—bare of ornamental accessories, pictures, or plants, and yet was functional, airy, and spotlessly clean. We were greeted at the door by a *Bauersfrau* (peasant woman) in her late thirties. She had a husky, scrubbed, red-cheek look, and was decidedly unimpassioned, but correct. There were no men. I assumed they were all fighting in the war or dead. Hans never left the front entrance; he simply handed us over to the landlady like a commodity and disappeared. Nothing was explained.

I can only imagine the shock that greeted Mother at seeing that Klaus and I were not where she had left us just a few minutes before. She was told to continue on her way to America. They told her that she was still young and to go back home and start a new family and that she would soon forget about us. Mother went back to the hotel, cancelled our passage to the United States and returned to Hamburg. In Hamburg, she still had friends at the American Consulate which had not yet ceased operation and immediately sought assistance from her friend and supervisor, Consul General Alfred Ray Thomson. Although months of searching went by without a trace or clue as to our whereabouts, Mr. Thomson was thoroughly knowledgeable of political conditions in Nazi Germany and was able to use his influence and contacts to obtain information for Mother regarding our abduction. Mother returned to the American Consulate roll until it was closed on July 8, 1941. Months later on December 8, 1941, the United States declared war on Japan and entered battle with both Japan and Germany.

Through Mr. Thomson's contacts, Mother learned that the abduction was instigated by Vati and organized by the Gestapo to keep Klaus and me as German citizens. Our uncle provided the logical liaison. Mother also tapped another source, our good friend from Marxen, Georg Mikel-Garbers. Georg Mikel-Garbers's connection with the Nazi Party, combined with information learned through Mr. Thomson's research, provided a reasonable start for Mother to begin her search for Klaus and me.

After the consulate closed, Mr. Thomson was offered a position in Glasgow, Scotland, but suffered a nervous breakdown and returned to Washington. His mother, Anna R. Thomson, writes in her book, *Historical Letters* (New York: Hobson Book Press, 1946): "He arrived home a broken man. Although he was in the prime of life and fully able to serve his country in a most competent way, there was no post open. Not being able to shake off his deep despondency, he died a year and a half afterward." Mother made a note in the margin of Alfred Thomson's eulogy written by Ralph C. Busser, a retired Consul General: "Amen! He was an angel to Aurora Evans Ritter." She noted that he had a fine, genteel nature and took personal interest and care of his employees. Mother admired and respected Mr. Thomson for his unusual compassion and kindness and referred to him as "her true friend and a wonderful patriot." Mother continued corresponding with his mother and, later, with his sister, Harriet Gibbs, both of Washington, D.C.

Neither Klaus nor I knew where we were. The town and all the people were strangers to us. After Uncle Hans deposited us, the *Bauersfrau* took us to an attic room where we sat on a bed like two new puppets that had been put there on display. We were more bewildered than frightened. Soon several little children came into the room and tried to engage us in conversation and play. They were happy but curious and had no clue what was going on. All Klaus and I did was ask where our mother was and when she was coming to get us. The Bauersfrau repeatedly told us that Mother was going on to America and that we were going to stay in Germany. I never considered this a serious threat since Klaus and I felt secure that Mother would eventually find us. I did wonder all the time where she might be. I don't remember much more about our abduction or how we spent the days in "captivity." As I said, the house was neat, the food was sparse and unremarkable, the woman was correct and dependable like a robot, and the children were nice. No one was rude or ever threatened us. We were there for five months, and I'm totally blanked out on our daily activities except for the fact that we spent most of our days confined in the attic room. Besides the day of our arrival, only two other events clearly linger in my mind during the entire five months of our confinement. I remember the day Klaus entered school in Ratzeburg. I went along when the Bauersfrau took her children and Klaus to school. Each of the first-grade children carried the conventional *Tüte*, which is a large conical-shaped container that is constructed out of decorated cardboard and filled with candy and various toys and school supplies. All children entering first grade carry a Tüte with them to class on their first day of school. If Klaus received one for entering school in Ratzeburg, I'm not sure. The rest of the days just passed in a blur. I remember waiting on Klaus to come home and nagging the Bauersfrau about our mother. Ratzeburg was too far away from Hamburg or other large cities, ports, factories, or rail yards to be targeted by bombs. Like many of the villages and burgs in Europe, Ratzeburg featured historic buildings in the town center and farmlands fringing the circumference. Our neighborhood was neither city nor country—just typical monotonous subdivision architecture. As in all of Germany, there were sidewalks and small produce stores within a few minutes' walk. No cars were in sight anywhere. If a car came into our neighborhood, the adults rushed to the window and pressed their noses on the glass, yet hiding most of their faces and bodies behind the curtain. Nearly always, the word "car" was synonymous with Gestapo and meant trouble— an arrest, reprimand, or inquiry. All the tiny immaculately manicured front yards had picket fences and gates to the sidewalk. I didn't learn the name of the town until I was an adult. The atmosphere was stoic and somber for Klaus and me. We didn't sense anger or joy—our emotions were on hold—a mental and emotional vacuum. We continued asking about our mother. We always received the same answer: that she'd already left for America. We kept asking. We never played outdoors. I presume the neighbors might wonder where we came from. We ate dinner at the table downstairs with the host family and then went back upstairs. Most likely the Bauersfrau received compensation for confining us. Klaus and the other children regularly attended school in a small-town school building within walking distance. When Klaus wasn't doing his homework, we played with the resident children in our room. As mentioned, no one was ever mean to us—just firm. But I know we didn't laugh once in five months.

The third memorable day in Ratzeburg was the day I was whisked off to a neighbor's house. Klaus was in school. Landlady Bauersfrau came to our upstairs room all in a huff of excitement and, without explanation, yanked my hand and literally dragged me behind her as she bounded down the steps with me in tow. We dashed through the front door and turned right, continuing our pace along the sidewalk, until we reached her friend's house, two doors down the street. The Bauersfrau and I were met at the front entrance by her neighbor who quickly took charge of me. The transfer was swift, and little time was wasted on instructions. The Bauersfrau abruptly turned around and hastened back home. My new custodian gave no social introduction. She just grasped my hand and hustled me up the steps to a second-level bedroom just left of the stairs. She released me into the room and pulled the door shut behind her as she told me to stay quiet and not to make any noise or attempt to come out. Then she locked the door and fled back down the stairs. I was petrified; but at the same time, my heart was palpitating like an audible drumbeat; and I knew if something was bad for them, it must be good for me. I hovered by the door with one eye and one ear taking turns, pressing firmly to the keyhole of the highly shellacked wooden door. I heard and saw nothing. The house was eerily quiet. I don't think I was breathing.

After an indefinite time, the doorbell rang. My new lady custodian answered the door, and then I heard an exchange of voices. The conversation grew louder. A man was talking and then more women's voices. My new custodian shouted to these visitors that they could not enter since she had just finished waxing the floors and stairs. A highly charged argument ensued. I strained harder against the door. As the chorus of voices grew in volume and the excitement heightened, I was pretty sure I recognized my mother's voice. Hardly able to contain my anxiety, I banged both my fists on the door and yelled loud enough for Mother to recognize my voice. The angry exchange of words continued, but now the sound of quick footsteps was approaching up the stairs. Mother called out to me, and finally, reluctantly, the woman of the house unlocked the bedroom door, and I was in my mother's arms. We hugged and kissed and cried but had little time for a reunion since both Onkel Georg Mickel-Garbers and Mother were frantic to find Klaus and get out of town. I told them he was in school. We had to find our way to the schoolhouse. Mother and Georg kept asking me where the school was. I wasn't sure but remembered the direction we had walked from our house that first school day. Mother, carrying me, and Onkel Georg literally ran all the way through the streets until we spotted the building. It was a single-story rectangular brick building with a steeply pitched roof-line. The wide double front doors were at the narrow end, leading directly into a central corridor the width of a two-car garage—so it seemed to a small child. The hall continued the full length of the school building with another set of double-wide doors at the far end. The double doors in the back were closed. About half a dozen classrooms were on either side of the corridor except for the principal's office, which was midway down the hall on the right. I remembered that Klaus's class was the last room on the right. School was in session, but the hall was empty and dark as the three of us tried to tiptoe stealthily, and unnoticed, across the wooden boards to the end of the hall. Fortunately, all the classroom doors were shut except his. We stood slightly back and at an angle from his classroom door, avoiding the bright daylight cast through the open door. We stayed out of the teacher's line of vision as she was in front of the class. We saw Klaus sitting in his desk about two-thirds back near the windows.

Like all the other students, his head was bent over his work. No sound came from anyone in the room. We concentrated on Klaus and fixed on him to catch his attention without sound by wildly flinging our arms in the air. We were so focused that we never noticed if any of the other children saw us. Finally, Klaus looked in our direction. When he recognized Mother and Georg, he dropped his pencil, jumped out of his desk, and bolted out of the room. His path ran directly in front of the teacher. All of the kids were stunned and stared in disbelief. This type of undisciplined act would not go unpunished in German schools. The teacher called for Klaus to halt and charged after him into the hall. By now, all of us were halfway down the hall, fleeing toward the exit. The teacher yelled the principal's name as she ran past his office, and he too dashed out of his room and into the hall to join the chase. We were out the door and into the street before anyone could stop us. It was over. We were together again.

Klaus and I returned to Hamburg with Mother. Although Mother was our legal guardian, it did not mean we were free to leave Germany. She was called into court and severely reprimanded for attempting such a rash act as trying to take her children with her to America. If she made one more attempt to leave Germany, the judge pronounced, she would never lay eyes on her children again. After all, Germany was our Vaterland.

In the meantime, Mother had rented and furnished another apartment in Hamburg, Parkallee Ten, which was about three blocks from where we had lived before. She was newly employed as an accountant for Phrix-Werke Aktiengesellschaft, Hamburg 35, Phrix-Haus, Gehaltsbüro, a stockbroker-accounting firm and an affiliate of the Dresdner, Deutsche, and Commerzbank banks in Hamburg. She worked for Phrix from 5 August 1941 until 31 December 1943. We lived on the ground floor on Parkallee and had a small courtyard in front—to the right—just as one approached the wide granite entrance stairs. Our apartment was the first door on the right after entering the hotel-sized foyer. The door of our apartment opened into a long hall that stretched along the left wall directly into a galley kitchen at the back. The kitchen was compact but basic and functional. It had one small window that opened onto the inner court and a *Speisekammer* (a larder closet). Next to the kitchen was the bathroom. Then we had a large bedroom where all three of us slept. We had two twin beds pushed together in the middle of the room and one single bed along the wall. All the ceilings were at least ten feet high or more. Two wide sliding doors separated the living/dining area from the bedroom. The gigantic doors were ceiling to floor and pushed into the wall on each side, creating a near-ballroom-size living/sleeping space. A complete gym set with swing, rings, and pull-up bars was attached to the support beam between the bedroom and living/dining area. It was constructed out of rope and beautifully finished wood and could be rolled up so the sliding doors could be shut for privacy. We were able to swing as easily and far out between rooms as one could on a playground. The indoor gym set provided basic calisthenics for Klaus and me during the countless inclement days in Germany. Moving to the front of the apartment from the living room was a glassed-in veranda, which opened to a small porch that had steps leading down to the front garden bordering the sidewalk. The yard was tiny but beautifully kept with flowers and surrounded by a wrought-iron fence. Mother had planted two giant sunflowers on each side of the little porch. There was another room to the right of the apartment entrance which Mother rented to a single lady to defray expenses. Many of the consulate employees who fled sold or gave to Mother their furniture. Our beds were brass with inlaid mahogany and the two wardrobes in our bedroom were mahogany and ebony. Our living-room floor was covered with a magnificent carpet from Smyrna of bright blues and reds. I particularly loved the dining-room tablecloth. It was black silk with gold fringe, and painted in the center was a bright peacock carefully detailed in brilliant colors outlined in gold. The peacock almost sprang to life with its lustrous plumes. Also, from the ceiling of our living room hung an exquisite chandelier—which the three of us together polished, crystal by crystal. This was a coordinated effort. One person stood on the ladder, unhooking and handing down each crystal. Another person washed the crystal, and the last of us dried each piece and returned it to be hung. The furniture in the veranda was from Budapest. It was constructed of inlaid wood and hand painted a soft yellow and light green. The cushioned circular bench fit into the corner of the veranda—almost like a built-in. The matching set included a table and cabinets. When we were at home, we spent most of our time on the veranda. Hamburg can be dreary, particularly in winter, and the natural light or occasional sunshine spreading through the large glass panels was warm and friendly, and our bodies turned to the light like the face of a flower to the sun. Our pets also enjoyed the warmth and light of the veranda. They consisted of two canaries and a tank full of goldfish and snails.

The following map indicates the relationship of our and Vati's homes—all in the Harvestehude section of Hamburg. Our first home, Heinrich-Barth Strasse, is number 1. Parkallee, the home that was bombed, is number 2. And, Rothenbaumchaussee is number 3 where Vati and Irmgard lived with her grandmother. The properties are located northwest of the city center, near the Alster pavilion and the Rathausmarkt.

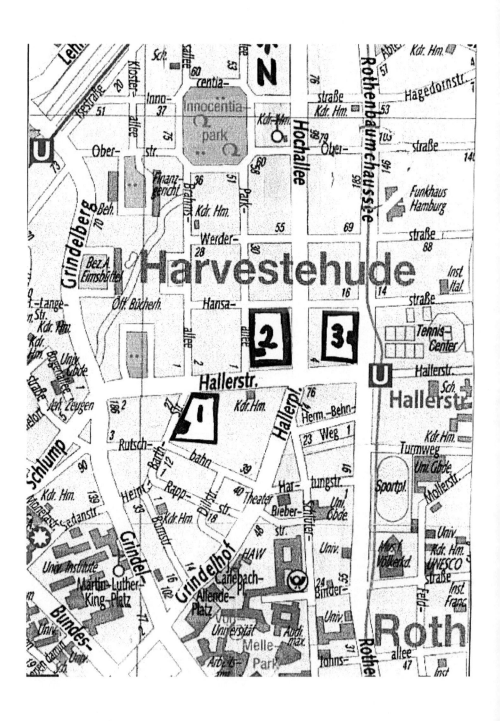

Our home at Parkallee was elegant and cheerful, and I was so happy to be reunited with Mother. But it was also the home where I saw a dead person for the first time and where I realized that there was suspicion and fear of evil lurking about outside of our home—besides our personal abduction. The three of us were in our apartment when we heard an ambulance or wagon pull up in front of the building. As we went to our front door to see what was happening, we also detected murmuring of voices in the lobby right outside our door. Mother cautiously opened the door to check what the disturbance was about just as the medics were rolling a gurney out of our neighbor's apartment. The gurney had a body on it. It was the old man who had lived by himself directly across the lobby from us. Several people from our building were standing, obviously ill at ease, while watching the commotion. No one said he was Jewish. But the old gentleman had committed suicide, so we were told. Klaus and I didn't even know the word "Jew," but somehow, the fact that he wanted to take his own life made it clear that he was afraid and preferred not to live. We rarely saw the old man, but I remember that he was small, partially bald, had a goatee, and walked stooped over. Most of the time, when I saw him, he wore a hat. I'm sure Mother suspected why he killed himself. It was a somber interruption in our daily routine. Mother quietly closed the door. Without saying, we knew by the troubled look on Mother's face and her pained demeanor that this was an episode not to be discussed. And we didn't.

Except for police dogs, large pets like cats and dogs were not popular during the war because food was so scarce. Slaughtered dogs and horses were sold on the black market. I recall being told that horse meat tasted uncommonly sweet, but it was never a consideration in our household. On rare occasions, we saw a neighbor who had a white spitz. I was dying to pet his fluffy white fur coat, but the spitz was too arrogant and unfriendly. Unaccompanied German shepherds were used liberally to guard entrances to restricted commercial, government, or public property. Once, Mother, Klaus, and I were stopped by a German shepherd. He was left unattended and loose at a guard station. It was late evening, and we wanted to take a shortcut through a fenced industrial yard. The area was relatively well lit, but we didn't see the dog and walked right through the gate when we heard ferocious barking and snarling behind us.

We snapped to attention. In no time, the large German shepherd blocked our way. Mother said for us to freeze and stay calm. We froze but didn't stay calm since that's easier said than done when eye to eye with a snarling beast. Klaus and I didn't move because we weren't breathing. Mother just kept reassuring us in a low voice that the dog just needed to sniff us. It seemed like an eternity, but the shepherd inspected each of us meticulously before he backed away and then slowly headed back to his post. We also proceeded slowly and stealthily on our way. I always wondered what the dog smelled about us that triggered him to retreat.

Mother had several good friends in the Parkallee area. Frau Becker, who lived in a townhouse one block from us, was one of her regular acquaintances. Frau Becker's husband had been killed in the war and she was raising her only child, a son, Dieter. Dieter was about our age. He and Klaus sometimes played with their little magnet cars and made them stick to the streetlight poles, which were made of iron. He was a nice little kid but could be mischievous. Typically of Dieter, he once played a trick on us and told us to say, "Die Hüner picken [The chickens peck]." Then he told us to repeat that sentence but, this time, say it while we pull with our fingers on each side of our mouth to stretch our lips taut. Well, try it and see what happens to the sound of the letter p. Of course, that changed the meaning of what the chickens were doing. We were surprised but took some satisfaction in saying the F word without guilt.

I loved our Parkallee Ten apartment. It is the place in Germany I remember most as home. Like the expanded Ritter family, we attended the Lutheran Church in Hamburg whenever they had services. It was a majestic old church with high stained-glass windows that had exquisitely carved and painted symbols, icons, and human figures in color that one could easily incorporate into their daydream while the minister was preaching on and on. I was baptized in Verden an der Aller in my grandmother's baptismal dress. The Ritter genealogy lists my grandparents as evangelical. The Evangelical Church of Germany is a union of all protestant churches, creating an alliance of independent churches of various protestant denominations.

Christmas at Parkallee, as all our Christmases in Germany, was a truly euphoric and romantic ritual as well as a religious experience.

Despite political tension and military restrictions, department stores tried their best to fulfill expectations of festivities. However, one had to stand in line for hours just for the most mundane items. Of course, there were no super markets; so we stood in line at the bakery; the dairy, the butchers, the produce market, and the cheese counter to purchase our daily food. We also had to wait in line to watch movies at the Kino. Standing in line was part of the German war culture. In fact, you never expected not to stand in line. "Line standing" took on a life of its own, and you simply planned it into your daily schedule. It was an anticipated and accepted way of life. There was relatively little interaction among those making up the silent slowly forward-creeping human chain. Mostly, no one spoke because, if they were standing outdoors, they were frozen stiff and couldn't unclamp their jaws, or they didn't want to lose body heat through the mouth. Also, it is not common among Germans to converse with strangers, and the political dynamics at the time made verbal interaction unsafe.

The holiday season, especially Christmas, exacerbated the time one had to spend standing in lines. I remember that on one particular Christmas, we were upstairs in a department store, waiting near the end of a fifty-foot line just to buy one pack of tinsel for our tree, when one of Mother's friends, Herr Sepp Ostermayer, happened to walk by. He was a funny character. He said, "Hi, what are you standing in line for?" Mother told him, "Tinsel." He said, "Just a minute. I'll get you some." In his customarily casual fashion, Sepp sauntered to the head of the line like he owned the store and without hesitation handed the sales clerk some money and informed her that he needed a pack of tinsel. She was so taken aback that she sold him the package without hesitation. Herr Ostermayer took the tinsel and walked away as all the people in line scrutinized him, wondering who he was. I was so impressed with his brass. We were eternally grateful for those two hours saved. Sepp Ostermayer was a jokester. He always made Mother and us laugh. Herr Ostermayer was a caricaturist and regularly sketched funny cartoons of us—such as Klaus posing like a cowboy or Mother impersonating Carmen, dancing with a rose in her mouth. I don't know why he wasn't a soldier. Sepp was the only man we knew of eligible military age and no obvious excuse for not fighting. He was unmarried and had no visible handicaps. As adults, we learned that Mother suspected he was homosexual. Of course, under no circumstance would she express this thought to us—especially since we had no clue what that meant.

We never had air raids during Christmas. I believe it is a carryover of the Christmas truce of World War I. I read in the *Washington Post* on December 25, 2004, the following article regarding the "Christmas truce":

> Nobody knows where the Christmas Truce of 1914 began . . . What is known is that 90 years ago today—four months into what would eventually be called World War I—thousands of British, French, and Belgian soldiers spent a cold, clear, beautiful Christmas mingling with their German enemies along the Western Front. The mysterious beginnings are fortunate. For want of the name of the first person (probably German) who proposed fraternization, or the place where it occurred (probably somewhere in Flanders), the Christmas Truce has acquired the aura of a miracle. In lacking a hero or sacred site, it has kept a single emotion at its core—the desire for peace of the most literal and personal kind.

The article goes on to say that they buried one another's dead and took care of the wounded together. They exchanged food and, in some cases, alcohol; sang songs; and traded cigarettes. The German government sent candles and small Christmas trees to the troops, and the British received pipe tobacco and candy. They spoke mostly in English and frequently played games like kickball. The truce was observed almost everywhere, beginning Christmas Eve, which is holy for the Germans.

Apparently, though not official, there was an unspoken mutual respect for the "holy day." Christmas in Germany has always been shrouded in mystery. Children do not participate in decorating the tree. The tree is behind closed doors or hidden by a divide. Only at midnight of December 24 will the "vale" be lifted. We children nearly erupted with anticipation. On the first day of December, we lit candles for Kris Kringle, Santa's helper, and left sweets on the windowsill for him. In turn, we might find a little gift on the sill. Also, the home had an Advent wreath and Advent calendar. The wreath had four candles, and each Sunday in December, we lit one candle until all four were burning by Christmas Day.

Christmas celebration in Germany begins with late dinner the evening of the twenty-fourth. We all wore our finest formal dress clothes. Mother always donned a long evening dress for the occasion. Dinner was served promptly at 10:00 p.m. The table was set with the finest china, crystal, and sterling; but the food was humble and consisted mostly of potatoes, red cabbage, dumplings, maybe sauerbraten if available, and a simple pudding for dessert. Candy during wartimes was predominately crystallized sugar, licorice, and maybe gummy bears. Good chocolate was not readily available. Our grandmother sent us homemade marzipan balls rolled in powdered chocolate and ginger cookies sometimes dipped in chocolate. Even the marzipan was mixed with thickly cooked cream of wheat to stretch the almond paste. It was a tradition for Santa Claus to come to the home and visit children on Christmas Eve. Mother always engaged a professional or friend to dress the part and surprise us. Santa asked us if we had been good boys and girls, and we told him yes and recited a little poem that every German child knew. The words of the verses translate to "Dear kind Santa Claus, please put your switch away because we've been very good." Santa Claus might *ho ho ho* a bit with us, ask us "planted" questions as if he knew all about us, and then give us a small gift and leave. Herr Myers was our most reliable Santa Claus for many years. However, he was not available one Christmas and Mother had to hire a substitute. As we were going through our ritual, Santa started crying uncontrollably. Klaus and I were in shock. He completely broke down and said that our home and tree were so beautiful and that he had lost his wife recently and the ambiance reminded him of home. We had not even realized that Santa Claus was married.

The men who performed as Santa Claus always visited Mother a day or two before the event to receive specific instructions on what to say and to get paid. On another jolting Christmas Eve, Sepp Ostermayer came by for a visit early Christmas Eve day and chatted with Mother. I was still greatly impressed with his bold and chivalrous purchase of our tinsel. My eyes scrutinized this hero with painstaking precision as he and Mother talked. That same eve, directly before midnight, we heard a knock on the door and Santa Claus entered. We began going through our ritual, reciting poems and telling Santa Claus how wonderful we were, when all of a sudden, Santa's shoes caught my eyes. And wouldn't you know, they looked exactly like Sepp Ostermayer's—brown on white, like golf shoes with the little holes in the brown leather. I looked up at him and said, "You're not Santa Claus; you're Herr Ostermayer." He looked at Mother to bail him out, but she just laughed. It was disappointing but not particularly traumatic for us. I think we knew all along that some guy was wearing a suit, but sometimes it's nice to be caught up in a fantasy.

Holy Eve begins at precisely midnight on the twenty-fourth of December. Someone rings a little bell, and the door to the Christmas-tree room opens. All the electric lights in the room are off. Only the glow of the flickering tree candles illuminates the room. The dainty glass decorations reflect the light from the candles, and each single strand of carefully hung tinsel shimmers as it sways freely from each branch. Gifts lie unwrapped under the tree. It was a dazzling and wondrous sight. Klaus and I presented Mother with our little self-made, carefully wrapped gifts that we had whispered about in secret for so long. Or our gift might be a poem, song, or piece of instrumental music. It was not uncommon for children to present parents with a show of their talents—encouraged and supported by the schools. Holy night was shrouded in wonderment and mystery. Christmas was a complete package in itself including the participants with all the adornments. We were the characters in a romantic pageant play.

Our Santa Claus, Herr Myers

Mother with Klaus and Me

SCHOOL AND BOMBS

I like to think that I have inherited the ability to survive
as our forefathers survived the disastrous journey from
England to the New World. Man is made of stern stuff.
Getting food, heating frigid homes, protecting helpless children—
these occupy people even when bombs rain down.
A. E. Ritter, *Murmurings.* p. 75.

TYPICALLY, IN PEACETIME, elementary-school children attend school until noon six days a week with at least two hours of homework assignments. During the war—depending, of course, where in Germany you lived—classes were scheduled and cancelled according to air-raid forecasts, available shelters, the proximity of combat, and sometimes just battle rumors. The less we attended school, the more homework we were assigned. Our classroom was arranged similarly to most American classrooms: chalkboard in front and wooden desks arranged in neat rows. We were assigned a seat in no particular order. Roll was called each morning. We said our pledge to the German republic and sang the national anthem, "Deutschland, Deutschland, Über Alles" (Germany, Germany, over All). I don't recall that we said Heil Hitler in class. Like most of Mother's friends, nearly all of the schoolteachers were intellectuals and didn't share Adolf Hitler's ideology, yet nothing was ever spoken for fear of an informant. It was not too difficult to distinguish between Hitler's supporters and nonsupporters. His disciples expressed blunt defense for the Reich and scorn and malevolence toward adversaries. The school curriculum emphasized the three *R*s with alternating weeks for music and art classes. Reading, writing, and mathematics were drilled. Arithmetic focused on memorization of the multiplication tables through the number twenty. This meant fast answers of any combination of the tables through twenty, which, of course, results in instant recognition of division and square-root numbers as well. There was no such thing as long division. All math had to be done from memorization. A fifth grader was expected to be completely proficient in any combination of the numbers one to twenty. Also, we used our ruler and other tools for many practical applications such as measuring furniture, books, walls, etc. in the classroom as well as features like fences, walls, posts on the playground. Writing was strictly penmanship, and the emphasis was on perfection. No erasing, smearing, or tearing in the paper were allowed. Our written work was done in ink. If we turned any paper in with an error, we had to rewrite the entire page until it was perfect. This was accomplished either at home or after school. Reading was conducted the same way. We had to read paragraphs or stories over and over again at home to be able to read them perfectly in class. No faltering was tolerated. I'm not saying we were spanked if we made mistakes, but it reflected on our grades. Perfection through repetition was the motto of our schools. If all of this sounds harsh, it gave us a sense of satisfaction and accomplishment but lacked the freedom of creativity. Creative thought was not encouraged. All emphasis was on discipline. Even if we had to copy a page over and over until perfect, we were proud to turn a perfect paper in to the teacher. It looked good even if we didn't know or care what we were writing. Our schools had little history or geography in the lower grades.

Our intellect in school was stimulated through music and art, definitely not original reading, writing, or oral expression. When a man with a violin entered our room, we knew it was time for our music lesson. He distributed pages of notes and words—not always on the same page. As he played the violin, we learned how to listen, read notes and distinguish tone and pitch, and sing. Arts and crafts were taught in another building. Art was my favorite class. Typically, the boys had woodwork shop or machine shop, and the girls learned drawing but mostly crafts. Supplies were provided by the school system, and all art projects were stored at school until fully complete. We were taught the importance of doing one project well rather than

180 throwaway doodads. The tasks were of our original designs and were produced well enough to give to our parents for Christmas. Likewise for boys. Sometimes we worked an entire year on one primary object. For example, girls learned how to sew; cross-stitch; knit; weave; and braid (cloth, paper, and leather); paint on glass; mold clay; cut black-paper silhouettes; and embellish silhouettes with colored transparent tissue paper. We always framed our drawings or cutouts and finished all projects in such a way as to create a presentable product. We used potato prints or paints to design our own wrapping paper. I remember being positively excited as I worked on my gifts. I could hardly wait for a birthday or Christmas to arrive in order to show Mother what I had made for her. Speaking of Christmas, we also had to learn a poem or song in school each year to present to our parents. Children didn't have money, and certainly, no one received allowances. So one way to give was to give of ourselves—however humble. For the rest of our lives, whenever we asked our mother what she wanted, she always said, "Something that you make," or, when we were older, "I just want to hear you and Klaus play the piano and the violin." Franz Schubert's "Ave Maria" was her favorite. The school day did not include any physical-education classes. We spent so few hours in school that we were lucky to get bathroom breaks. With the exception of monsoon rains and snow blizzards, we were instructed to run, top speed, back and forth between the school building and back fence of the school grounds. This exercise probably took fifteen minutes before we went back inside.

The German school system requires thirteen grades for graduation. After the fourth grade, all children are eligible to take an examination that determines whether they can continue their education in a college preparatory curriculum or vocational school curriculum. One must pass the test in order to take college preparatory classes. The student may hire a tutor or repeat fourth grade and take the test again. Also, students may opt not to take the exam if they prefer to go into a specific vocational profession such as baking, electronics, mechanics, carpentry, sewing, etc. Either way, all pupils must complete thirteen grades. Students who graduate with a vocation are highly skilled and considered professionals. Vocational students may also continue their specialized training and perfect their skills to earn the title of master, such as master baker, master carpenter, etc. We happened to be in a pub when a carpenter celebrated his Master's certificate with his pals. Almost all high-school graduates in Germany speak English or at least one foreign language. Klaus passed the college preparatory exam and began studying English in fifth grade.

So far, many of the air raids still came during the night, and for the first and second grades, we attended school somewhat regularly. However, second grade was a disaster for me. I knew the teacher didn't like me, and my grades reflected her hatred. We didn't know why. I complained to Mother, but we had no proof of prejudice. Her vengeance against me continued to grow. She sought the slightest opportunities to punish or embarrass me. When I had a nosebleed, she made me lay on the floor in front of the room directly under the portable chalkboard. She openly made fun of me in class. The climax came when she slapped me so hard on the cheek that I still had the swelling and imprint of her fingers on my face when Mother came home from work. Mother was furious, and the next day, she charged into the principal's office and said she'd had enough of the teacher's physical and emotional abuse as well as my failing grades. To me, embarrassment in front of the class and poor grades were worse than the punishment. The principal was most sympathetic and apologetic. He explained to Mother that he was aware of my teacher's prejudice and hatred of foreigners. Her son and husband had been killed in the war, and she released her bitterness through me for having an "enemy" for a mother. He said that teachers were difficult to find, and he hired her out of sympathy and necessity. This didn't make me feel any better, but I was relocated to another second grade where I survived under reasonable circumstances. Having an American mother didn't make Klaus and me popular among our peers, especially when the kids noticed her accent. There were so few foreigners around that, if noticeable, they became the subject of scrutiny by all. However, most of the adults with whom Mother interfaced in day-to-day business displayed no animosity or negative reactions to her nationality. In fact, despite America being the enemy of the German government, the average German citizen loved America and the American people.

The following school picture was taken in my Gross-Flottbek school. I'm standing in the third row from the front and fourth from left.

My fourth grade class in front of our arts and crafts building

I don't recall that attending school was ever routine or predictable or that the length of the school day was certain. Every week, every day, and even every hour of classroom attendance was dependent on safety, which was determined by local air-raid warnings. When the United States began providing bombing support to England and eventually joined the war, daylight air raids became more common. The British night attacks on individual targets were not precision enough to make a significant impact on the war, hence they switched to area bombing over an entire city. It was the Americans with their B-17 Flying Fortress bombers who introduced formation daylight raids. No one was safe beneath their hail of bombs which rarely lasted over half an hour at a time. However, as the Allied fighters became more proficient, air attacks came in waves—again and again on the same city. We lived in a full-scale combat zone—raids at day and night. During our first and second year in school, we attended classes somewhat regularly. Prior to the sirens, alerts usually came by radio or, many times, by rumor. I don't believe schools were alerted ahead of the general public. Scuttlebutt from Mother's office or gossip from a neighbor usually informed us that another air raid is due in a day or two and where it might be expected to hit. This was much like our news today of forthcoming storms or hurricanes. If we happened to be in school already when the first sirens warned of enemy aircraft heading in our direction, school closed, and we were scooted out in a hurry to get home. Sometimes, we made it home before we heard the second and final siren. At other times, we were not so lucky, and we'd get caught by the final siren as we ran toward home. This meant business, and we had to dart into a private residence or public shelter immediately. We were always sent home. We never stayed in a shelter at school. As the war intensified, you could already hear the engines of the planes when the final sirens sounded imminent alert. All of a sudden, the street scene was paralyzed. Pedestrians disappeared into homes or shelters. The stillness was frightfully eerie and unnerving. Like stepping outdoors after a heavy snowfall, time freezes in place: no cars, no lights, no animals, few people (all rushing to find cover), and just the bombers buzzing slowly in formation overhead like a dark blanket covering the city—a swarm of killer bees. Of course, as always, we listened for the first sound of a bomb whistling down upon us to assess the proximity. Occasionally, the squadrons hummed right on over and faded into the distance to unload their cargo on some other destination. On those rare occasions, fleeing schoolchildren heard the all-clear signal before they reached home. Those were the good days since we never had to turn back to school. We had the rest of the day off—frequently without homework. There was also a separate siren for bombs that were thought to contain poison gas. All of us were issued gas masks and instructed on how to secure them so no gas could get around the sides of the mask. Training included propaganda about the Russians using gas. We always were afraid of the Russians, never the British or American people. Gas masks were graphic and quite scary, and in the long run, I dreaded the possibility of being gassed more than being hit by a bomb. I had seen some frightening pictures of people who were gassed. Besides, gas masks looked intimidating, and I was afraid of seeing myself and others wearing such hideous green rubber masks. Luck didn't work with poison gas like it did with dodging conventional bombs.

To the Germans, the Soviets had a reputation for cruelty and torture. In an article "Ghost Ship," by Marcin Jamkowski in the February 2005 *National Geographic* issue, he writes:

German residents knew all too well what an encounter with the incoming Soviet Army could mean, having heard the story of Nemmersdorf, a village in East Prussia overrun by the Soviets the previous autumn. There the Red Army had taken bloody revenge for three years of suffering caused by the German invasion of Russia. After seizing the village, the soldiers had first raped all women, regardless of age, then had crucified them on doors of barns and houses. Men and children had been clubbed to death, shot, or run over with tanks . . . . German theatres were soon showing a horrifying newsreel filmed in the village.

Nemmersdorf was not the only captured town to meet such fate. There were many others across Germany. Germany was at fault, of course, for inciting the tiger. To say the least, to the German population, a hailstorm of bombs met with no greater fear than to be caught by a Soviet invasion. One of their torture camps was uncovered and made available to the public for viewing. Unfortunately, when we went inside the abandoned prison camp, we had no idea of what we would find. To the best of my recollection, it was partially underground. One particular form of Soviet torture displayed in the camp haunted me for many years. It was a closet built the same depth, height, and width of one person—like a vertical coffin. The inside of the closet door had a gigantean solid wooden street-cone-sized cone affixed to it. The sharp point of the cone, facing inward, was the same depth as the closet, and when the door was shut, the point touched the back wall of the closet. The intent was to force a person into the closet and then slam the door shut, jamming the sharpened cone through the body. I don't even remember the other torture devices, but that particular image is one of the few terrifying visual impressions left in my mind. This was a slip-up since Mother was consistently vigilant regarding any potential exposure Klaus and I might have to terror. It was also rumored that when German prisoners were being starved to death in Russian prison camps, they began eating the leaves on the trees in the camp. The Soviets then dusted the trees with poison, killing the famished prisoner in the camp. Despite the continuous bombings by the British and Americans, few Germans seemed afraid or bitter toward their English-speaking enemy. The French were never an issue.

As war progressed and intensified early in 1943-45, strategically located enemy air—and ground-force bases were established on the European continent, permitting quicker and deadlier destruction. Consequently, in many instances, German civil-defense operations did not receive adequate forewarning. Rather than risk trapping children in school and splitting families, we rarely attended school. School closings were announced by radio. We adjusted to the tempo of war. Nothing was predictable anymore. Some months, we had no school at all. Usually, we just assembled outside the school building at a designated place for each class. Our teacher collected homework, returned graded lessons, and handed out new assignments—always stressing reading, penmanship, and mathematics. I remember nearly freezing to death on the school grounds, waiting for our teacher to take the roll call and give the next day's instructions. One couldn't simply skip school without an excuse. The twenty or thirty minutes of standing still, in a straight line no less, on those bitter, cold, bleak days with the ground frozen solid and bits of snow twirling in the biting wind canceled any joy we might have had of going back home after our assignments. I recall how everyone's *Hauche* (breath) clouded the frigid air surrounding each line of students. It seemed forever before my body temperature returned to normal after I arrived home. Somehow, all of that seemed ordinary. No one ever protested. In the winter of '41, Mother often mentioned seeing disfigured young soldiers returning from Russia as she came through the train station. She said their frozen nubs were bandaged; noses and ears gone; and their weary, torn, emaciated bodies barely moving.

Frostbite was a common occurrence during the cold German winters. Klaus almost turned into an ice statue during one of our sled rides to the store. Mother kept telling us to move our fingers and toes, but after a while, they locked stiff and wouldn't move, and weariness set in. By the time we arrived home, Klaus was rigid, and his hands and feet were blue and numb as if with rigor mortis. Mother worked carefully for a long time to return circulation to the flesh of his brittle phalanges.

We lived on Parkallee for nearly three years. During the early 1940s, bombing targets were still mostly military installations, ports, and industries. The civilian population in cities and small villages were spared for the most part until 1942, though occasional mishaps occurred especially if one lived near the center of a metropolis as we did.

STRAFING

Living in the midst of the Second World War could
hold no happiness. The horror was emphasized since
we could not believe that this was the war to end wars.
I, myself, hate wars with a frightening passion because
I feel so positively that the makers of wars never fight
them. Counting victory by bodies torn to shreds
seems utterly senseless. A. E. Ritter, *Murmurings,* p. 76

ORIGINALLY, OUR VISITS to Marxen and Jesteburg were only on the weekends. But as the war continued, so did our stay on the farms. I have fond memories of the German countryside. It was, literally, a breath of fresh air in more ways than one. The heather country was rich in color, the farmhouses were neat, and the miles of wheat fields dotted with beautiful red poppies and blue cornflowers waved like a flag against the crisp horizon. We always looked forward to seeing the Unteutsch and Mikel-Garbers families. Marxen and Jesteburg lay in the midst of heather country a couple of hours south of Hamburg. For Klaus and me, visiting on the farm was a great vacation, but not without responsibilities. Each of us was assigned farm chores. If you eat, you work. For a while yet, we left the war in the city. On occasion, we heard the adults talking about rampages and local atrocities. During the latter years of the war, after the United States entered, there was no safe haven anywhere. Although the countryside was not a specific target for bombs, other isolated incidences plagued villagers and their farmlands. Children froze to death going from farmhouse to farmhouse or walking to and from school. War interrupts routine. I remember a particular incident when a young girl was caught by a snow storm on her way home from a neighbor's house. She had cut through the woods on her way home and lost her bearing made uncertain by wind-whipped snow. The entire community searched for her. She was found huddled near the base of a large tree—frozen to death. She just relaxed and went to sleep, all the people said. It doesn't really hurt and is not a bad way to die, the adults consoled themselves. Also, in order to incite foreign laborers to rebel against their landlords, British planes dropped small fuse incendiary packets to foreign workers with instructions on how to use them in sabotage operations (BRADDOCK II). By the time the war ended, the enemy air forces had dropped nearly six billion burn packets that scattered across farmlands. Of this number, three and a quarter billion were distributed between 6 June 1944 and 8 May 1945. The packets looked like two-to-three-inch, flat silver squares with a puffy middle—like a little handy wipe. When word came around that these had been dropped on the fields, schools closed, and children and adults held hands and combed the farmlands to collect the explosive bundles. Klaus and I saw many of these packets when we were in Jesteburg and were warned against playing with them. There were some reports of minor explosions and firecracker-like burns to children's eyes and hands. To my knowledge, they were not effective weapons against civilians and I never heard of any foreign worker in our area use them against their landlord's property.

Another tactic employed against individuals was ground strafing by Allied fighter planes. British, American, and Russian single pilot aircraft were encouraged to focus on anything that moved on the ground. This could be cars, trains, civilians, animals, etc. It was not until early 1945 that this became a popular "sport." Our family, seeking a safe haven on the farm, was not excluded. These fighter planes were originally commissioned to protect bomber formations from the German Messerschmitts that caused heavy casualties to the Royal Air force bombers and American B-17s.

I clearly recall two personal attacks by strafe planes. While in Jesteburg, we didn't have enough milk for the evening meal, so one of the Unteutsch girls and I set out with empty milk cans to fetch milk from a neighboring farm. It was not uncommon during the war for neighbors to exchange, barter, or give food. On our return from the milk mission, we were happily strolling down the center of a wide country dirt road, swinging our full milk cans, when we heard the engine of a single plane rapidly approaching behind us at near treetop altitude. But the trees were high, and we didn't see anything until it popped up from behind the woods and was so low that we could see the pilot's head. As he nose-dived his aircraft toward us like a swallow after a bug, we stumbled over each other, getting out of the way. Just then we heard the rat-a-tat popping of the machine gun and saw the bullets spatter into the dusty trail directly where we had walked. Each bullet splattered sand into the air like pebbles thrown into a lake. It all happened so unexpectedly. We fell into a shallow ravine under sparse brush, hoping to be invisible. We wondered if he might return to finish us off; but at the same time, it was over in a flash; and we figured if he really wanted to shoot us, we most certainly gave him an easy target. After we composed ourselves, we exhaled, and slowly inched our shaky bones into the open and ran home like two crazies. I think our sweet milk was churned to buttermilk by the time we reached our farm. After relating our adventure to the adults, our angst disappeared as quickly as it came. I had no concept of anyone wanting to kill me. Subconsciously, I thought the pilot had made a mistake. I realized other people were killed all the time, but that didn't apply to me. On another occasion, there were about four of us kids walking from Jesteburg to another village to purchase flour from the local miller when we heard a couple of single-engine planes approaching from behind. Fighter planes are easy to detect since they are small, fast, and travel only one or two together. They plunge as close to their target as possible. If you're in an open area, of course, you can see the planes coming and run in a zigzag pattern or dash for cover. On the road with houses, hills, or trees, they are difficult to spot until they're nearly on top of you. After the ground strafers sight their targets, they descend at 600 miles per hour from behind and open fire. Fortunately, we were at an advantage and heard and saw these two strafe planes coming for us. As the single-file bullets began pelting at our heels, we hurdled for the nearest tree cover along the road. We watched from the shadows of the trees as the second plane unloaded his machine gun. Again, the enemy disappeared as quickly as it came. It was over before we realized that we had been attacked. We barely had time to comprehend the danger. It's almost more like an annoying interruption, like an insult, rather than a life-threatening event. But nevertheless, for a few seconds, your heart cringes, and you hold your breath, listening for the approaching engine sound to return. When I think back on those experiences, I remember how intense the scare was and yet how quickly we recovered and took it in stride. It was just another day in the war zone. We went about our business as usual. I guess living with danger was the norm for us. We never knew anything except war, and as children under the age of eleven, we never considered death or injury as possibilities. Fright was just a reflex.

Winters in Germany are harsh. Temperatures stay near freezing without a single ray of sunshine while rain and dampness may hover for weeks without relief. During the cold days on the farm, meals were always served in a den area adjoining the kitchen, because it was the only room in the house that stayed heated all day—either from cooking or from a fire in the old-fashioned wood stove. Usually, kitchens in Europe are narrow, galley cooking areas. On farms, an eating area similar to today's family room typically adjoins the kitchen. This is where all the living activities took place in winter. This extended kitchen was the only place in the house where we didn't have to wear our heavy sweaters, so we usually lingered there until bedtime. It was just too cold to sew, read, or do homework anywhere in the house except in the kitchen vicinity. On the farm, bathrooms were rarely heated. We bathed in the kitchen. Klaus and I took turns being scrubbed down, head to toe, by standing in a large galvanized tub in the middle of the eating area. This event rarely took place more than once a week. However, we received a lot of daily face, hand, and neck scrubbing with plenty of soap and ice-cold water. Individual water heaters for the house were only lit on special occasions. We used water boiled on top of the wood stove for our baths. In the city, we had to rely on the apartment complex management to provide us with steam heat for the radiators. Property managers adhered to a strict energy ration schedule imposed by the government. Some days, there was no fuel, and our apartment was icy. Each tenant controlled his own water heater, but if the gas was turned off, we had nothing— not even hot water from the stove. Heat was always turned off at night and, if available, turned back on during meal times. Coal and peat were scarce, and we stayed warm by wrapping up in blankets and eating a lot of porridge and soups. Germans make soup out of nearly all edibles. Besides the meat S*peck* (bacon fat) and vegetable soups, and apple and potato soup (also called *Himmel und Erde* [heaven and earth]), we had recipes for beer, lemon, red—and white-wine, gooseberry, plum and prune, chocolate, rhubarb, rice, sweet-milk, and buttermilk soups. With our stomachs full of hot soup, we managed to raise our body temperatures enough to stay reasonably active. For sleeping, we had a feather bed under us and another plush down or feather "pillow" to cover over us. German feather beds were not like comforters with individually sewn down-filled pockets. The feather beds, shaped like one large pillow, covered the entire bed. We always slept warm and snuggly. It was just getting up in the mornings to a frigid room that was agonizing. When it was time to rise, we would wriggle under the cover to take our pajamas off and put on as many outer garments as possible without ever letting the cold air near our skin.

Except for special events, we changed our outer garments about once a week. The quality of our clothes, however, was excellent, and our shoes outlasted our growing feet. We had good woolens and thick cotton clothes. We layered anything that fit on top of other layers and whatever was warm. Style and color were inconsequential. We didn't wash our clothes regularly, but like with our bodies, Mother did a lot of spot cleaning. All holes were darned with whatever color and size yarn was obtainable. On the farm, we spun our wool and learned how to knit. When wool was not available, we could purchase an inexpensive artificial fiber for knitting. I still have a couple of pairs of mittens and caps we knit. Two of the mittens have five darned holes. A few other clothes that survived are Mother's black silk evening pajama bottoms she wore when our home was destroyed and one of Klaus's pajama tops. The frayed and fragile sleeves on the pajama shirt are held in shape by hundreds of darning stitches. I love looking at Mother's meticulously woven repairs. When you can't replace the old with the new, maintenance and mending are accepted as part of your culture. Mother also sewed her stockings. We threw nothing with potential away. And we found potential in all things. The saying "Penny-wise and pound-foolish" was not meant for a lifestyle without available replacement.

OPERATION GOMORRAH

*Our modern society tends to isolate people and foster loneliness,
but when disaster strikes, they may suddenly realize that the
little ugly duckling often saves the brood and is braver than
the peacock or the swan. World War II taught everyone in
bombing areas the value of the "little people." Close bonds
are formed when calamity strikes.* A. E. Ritter, *Murmurings*, p. 88

SIRENS, BOMBINGS, STRAFERS, burning, rubble, and death
were sights, sounds, and smells we grew up with. Ration cards, public
transportation, feeling cold, bomb shelters, and fear were anticipated
lifestyle and emotions that became routine to us—but which were
exciting. War is NOT dull. We never knew or coveted things of
materialistic, superficial opulence since we were never exposed to
them by word or in pictures. Out of necessity and also deliberation,
the German government made sure that our minds and emotions
did not yearn for the unattainable. We never went hungry and I don't
remember craving for delectables that didn't exist in my world. (I
think Mother had many nostalgic moments where she missed certain
foods more than clothing.) Clothes were only for warmth and if they
had any style to them it was a bonus. Fur coats were popular for
warmth, not prestige.

Mother refrained from speaking English to us or telling us of her
"ideal" childhood growing up in Alabama or of the good life in
America since it was best we never speak of these things with others
lest they suspect our allegiance to the United States and report us to
the authorities. We remained under casual surveillance.

Correspondence to Mother from family and friends in the States was severely censored, received months late, or never delivered at all. Until the war intensified around early 1943, we were still able to receive, on rare occasions, packages from family. Within a day or two after the arrival of a package (mostly coffee, sweets, cigarettes, and warm clothing), two young men in uniform (always two) from the Gestapo or Hitler Jugend would knock on the door, present themselves formally, and explain that they had received notification that we were recipients of a package from America. They explained that they had been instructed to inspect the contents of our parcel. The young men were always exceedingly polite and apologetic for the intrusion. Mother too was overly solicitous and offered to share anything in the package with them—sweets, coffee, etc. They always declined.

In Hamburg, late Friday night on July 23, 1943, Mother and her roomer were lounging on the small front terrace that lead out from our veranda. Mother had spent the day cleaning the apartment and preparing for our return. She took her bath, dressed in her black satin lounging pajamas and house shoes, and wrapped her washed hair in a silk scarf. As she and her boarder were relaxing and enjoying a rare cigarette in the pleasant July evening, a distinctly familiar overhead droning caught her attention. The hum came closer and stronger. Mother said to her friend, "These are not German planes; let's get inside and open the windows and head to the basement."

In Verden an der Aller, on Saturday morning July 24, 1943, nearing the end of summer vacation for Klaus and me, Oma, Annenie, Klaus, and I looked north, out through the veranda glass, and saw a deep crimson glow in the far-off horizon that swept upward into a sky made black by smoke. It looked like the other side of the world was on fire. All of us were focused toward the luminous reddening on the horizon. We were transfixed for what seemed a long time. Someone said, "I hope Aurora will be all right." This made Klaus and me anxious, but we didn't know what they meant. It never occurred to me that our mother would not be safe and live forever. Hamburg was being destroyed, and Mutti was in the midst of the inferno. Oma and Annenie had to know that Hamburg was being attacked.

Mother, like anyone who is accustomed to hearing large formations of bombers, recognized the quick repetitions and the wavy high/low sound vibrations of the rogue aircraft engines. This was not a German fleet of planes on a mission. This difference is especially noticeable when thousands of planes fly in formation overhead. No warning sirens had sounded, but Mother headed for the bedroom to unlatch the window to prepare for the worst. Radar communications had been intercepted by "Window", code name for strips of metal foil dropped by an aircraft to confuse enemy radar. It was a British invention designed to scramble German radar-detection systems, which also transmitted alerts to the siren stations. As Mother rushed to the back of the house to throw the bedroom window open (it was routine to open all windows to prevent implosion), the planes were already directly overhead; and she ran out the apartment, into the building foyer, and toward the basement steps. As she was about halfway down the steps, that dreaded whistle that bombs make when they slice through the atmosphere became louder and louder and ended with a deafening explosion in front of the house. Our once-elegant multistory apartment building, our home, furniture, and all our worldly possessions collapsed instantly into a pile of rubble, burying those who were already in the basement and killing and maiming the other tenants. It seemed like the world was coming to an end. The next wave of warplanes dropped phosphorous on the bombed city and turned Hamburg into an inferno. Fires were visible for 200 miles. The Royal Air Force (RAF) executed Operation Gomorrah in 48 minutes. It was the first operational use of "Window." Sunday, July 25th, while Hamburg is still burning, the United States Army Air Force (USAAF) bombed the city again in daylight. Wednesday, July 28, the RAF blitzed Hamburg again resulting in nine square miles of the city being set alight. On Friday, July 30, Hamburg is bombed one more time.

When I read Paul W. Tibbet's book, *Return of the Enola Gay*, I couldn't help but be roused as he describes the bomber formations as they leave the British island to fly to the European mainland. He said, "As the size of our raiding force gradually increased, squadrons from more areas across the English Midlands joined the morning takeoff ritual until the skies over the island literally echoed with the full-throated roar of many engines. It must have been heartening for the people of this beleaguered island to know that our aerial armadas were carrying the first waves of retribution to an enemy that had so recently visited destruction on London." I understand that retribution was an appropriate response to Hitler's aggressions. Yet, somehow being the recipient of these bombings for five years, it perplexed me that bombers loaded with tons of TNT, ready to kill and destroy human life, heartened one group of people and terrorized another group of people. I guess seeing this in print just impressed me with how juvenile and uncivilized war really is.

The following damage report of the raid in Hamburg, which was named Operation Gomorrah, is described by the United Strategic Bombing Survey, Summary Report (European War, September 30, 1945).

Early Air Operations—City Area Raids:

The pioneer in the air war against Germany was the RAF [Royal Air Force]. The RAF experimented briefly in 1940 with daylight attacks on industrial targets in Germany but abandoned the effort when [pilot] losses proved unbearably heavy. Thereafter, it attempted to find and attack such targets as oil, aluminum and aircraft plants at night. This effort too was abandoned; with available techniques it was not possible to locate the targets often enough. Then the RAF began its infamous raids on German urban and industrial centers. On the night of May 30, 1942, it mounted its first "thousand plane" raid against Cologne and two nights later struck Essen with almost equal force. On three nights in late July and early August 1943 it struck Hamburg in perhaps the most devastating single city attack of the war—about one third of the houses of the city were destroyed and German estimates show 60,000 to 100,000 people killed. No subsequent city raid shook Germany as did that on Hamburg; documents show that German officials were thoroughly alarmed and there is some indication from interrogation of high officials that Hitler himself thought that further attacks of similar weight might force Germany out of the war. The RAF proceeded to destroy one major urban center after another. Except in the extreme eastern part of the Reich, there is no major city that does not bear the mark of these attacks. However, no subsequent attack had the shock effect of the Hamburg raid.

An excerpt from the controversial Canadian documentaries *The Valour and the Horror* and *Death by Moonlight* by Brian and Terrance McKenna, author-producers, describes the lead-up to the attack on Hamburg and particularly the civilian population.

In a secret memo, October, 1942, Air Marshal Sir Charles Portal framed Bomber Command's new policy: "I suppose it is clear that the new aiming points are to be the buildup areas, not for instance, the dockyards or aircraft factories." In a meeting with the Chiefs of Staff Committee, Air Vice Marshal Harris (Sir Arthur Harris) enunciated his boss's policy: "We shall destroy Germany's will to fight. Now that we have the planes and crews, in 1943 and 1944 we shall drop one and a quarter million tons of bombs, render 25 million Germans homeless, kill 900,000 and seriously injure one million." The heyday of "area" bombing would be 1943. The bombers pounded Germany with 48,000 tons of explosives in 1942, and with another 207,600 tons in 1943. Night attacks escalated, targeting Germany's most populous regions: The Ruhr, March to June, 1943; Hamburg, July to November 1943 [when our home was destroyed]; Berlin, November, 1943 to March, 1944. John Terraine, a historian sympathetic to the RAF, described Bomber Command's new secret policy "as a prescription for a massacre, nothing more, nor less.

In our apartment building, anyone not buried in the basement was either crushed or burned to death. Mother was on the basement steps when the impact occurred. The steel and cement steps twisted and gave way under her feet. It was pitch-dark now. She heard screaming, choking, and gagging, as metal, bricks, and chalky, plaster dust were swirling and settling in the basement—depleting the oxygen. Many of the residents who made it to the basement or, out of habit were spending the night in the basement were either killed by falling ceiling and walls or choked to death. Moaning and screaming was all around. Family and friends were calling out names. Mother felt her way deeper into the basement. Fortunately, she had tied a silk scarf around her head. She took her scarf off and held it over her nose and mouth to filter the chalky particles created by the breaking-up of plaster and cement. Mother said the others took off their underwear or nightclothes to strain the dense air flow. If our apartment building had not had an exceptionally large Linden tree in front, Mother would have been dead on the spot. When the bomb made contact with the tree and detonated, the momentum and centrifugal force catapulted the mass into the front entrance of the building, causing its collapse. As were with many of the brick buildings, the outer walls frequently were the only part of the structure that remained upright. The inside went flat like a pricked balloon and lay heaped up in the center of the skeletal structures of the buildings. Also, if our apartment had not been on the ground floor and had Mother not recognized enemy planes and immediately left for the basement, she would have been crushed under the full weight of the building before reaching the basement. And if Klaus and I had been home, it would have taken us too long to get out of bed and grab a coat or blanket and get to the basement.

In the Martin Middlebrook's book *The Battle of Hamburg: The Firestorm Raid* (London, 1980), he writes:

> Hamburg air offensive. Employing WINDOW for the first time, to confuse German Radar defenses, the RAF committed over 3,000 bombers to four area bombing night raids on this German port: 24, 27, and 29 July and 2 August 1943. Additional nuisance raids were mounted and the US Army Air Forces also launched daylight raids on 25 and 26 July. The second night attack, which used high explosive and incendiary bombs alternately, caused the first manmade firestorm which affected an area of 22 sq. km. (8.5 sq. mi.). It rendered helpless the city's fire-fighting force and altogether it is estimated that the raids killed 44,600 civilians and 800 servicemen. It reduced half the city to rubble and nearly two thirds of what remained of the population had to be evacuated.

A firestorm is a solid wall of flames pushed forward by fierce wind. The wall of fire is created by incendiary bombs dropped after the city is already in rubble. This was a deliberate attempt at annihilating an area, including all life. The only three successful firestorms were in Hamburg in 1943 (when our home was destroyed), in Darmstadt in

1944, and in Dresden less than two months before the end of the war, 1945. In his book "Armageddon," Max Hastings writes that nearly two million homes were destroyed and 600,000 Germans perished. Two or three German civilians were killed by bombing for one German soldier on the battlefield. Chaos followed terror in the basement, where Mother and a half-dozen other residents tried to find a way out of the building before billowing flames smothered them. An underground garage was directly below our apartment, which made the garage adjacent to the basement. It is customary to keep shelters well stocked with sledgehammers, axes, water, medical supplies, and flashlights. The trapped tried to restore calm and order to plan an escape route. They concluded that knocking a hole through the garage wall would be their only option. They hoped to find a clear path for escape on the other side. For what seemed like hours, men and women beat, hammered, and clawed away in the darkness and confusion at the thick cement-and-brick wall in the foundation of the building until, piece by piece, the wall began to break-up, and the weary residents could see an opening developing. There was relief and renewed hope in discovering the space on the inside of the garage was relatively unobstructed. The few survivors from the great apartment building were able to crawl through the hole and proceed out of the garage into the street—unaware of the shock that awaited them. Once on the street, Mother said the sight of chaos and destruction was paralyzing and incomprehensible. She said it was like standing under a burning tent amid a deadly cross fire from flaming debris sailing through the air, blazing tree branches floating with the heat waves, and various explosions and implosions catapulting broken fragments of Hamburg's residential area across the scene like millions of shooting stars. Mother recalls a policeman on the street crying, "Hamburg is gone; the city is gone!" The heat was blistering, and the panic was unimaginable. As Mother stumbled through the burning obstacle course, she felt the heat through her thin house shoes, and her black silk pajamas were torn from crawling through the brick-and-mortar escape hole. The sight of blistered and parched people screaming and running in every direction without destination was horrific. Some, stupefied, were staggering across smoldering rubble, looking for family members. Many were paralyzed by what they saw and became demented, jabbering nonsense. Bodies and parts of bodies lay scattered among the smoldering debris. The mind could not register what the eyes were seeing. Mother told us that she looked at her hands and feet and said, "I'm rich." Black smoke and charred corpses against a red sky—a picture that could easily resemble a fundamentalist's rendition of hell. Screaming, moaning, and calling for help filled the air with horrible sounds of the dying—many on fire. The torturous heat and choking gases made it almost impossible to breathe. Mother said she just reminded herself to remain in control as she worked her way through the street to the house of a friend who lived several blocks from our home. She came to the place where once stood the home of one of her good friends. There she found a heap of rubble. Mother said she crawled on the wreckage and tried to dig in the debris, pulling up bricks, bent, hot metal pieces of wreckage, flinging and tossing debris wildly about to get down into the crater of the collapsed building all the while calling out her friend's name. She and others dug into the ruins with their bare hands and were able to uncover some corpses, but Mother never found her friend. She then carefully maneuvered her way to Mrs. Becker's house, the mother of Dieter, our friend. The Becker townhouse was partially standing, but both houses on each side were destroyed and burning. Mother was able to stand with Mrs. Becker as they watched her house slowly collapse and burn to the ground. She said her bruised feet and hands were burned, but she repeatedly expressed gratitude to be alive and in one piece and focused on the fact that Klaus and I were safe. The stench quickly became overpowering and revolting as corpses smoldered in the black smoke. Billowing fumes were dense with the rancor of charred flesh that made breathing a nauseating necessity.

"A Natural History of Destruction"—an article in the November 1, 2002, edition of the *New Yorker* by W. G. Sebald, translated from German by Anthea Bell—describes in detail the midsummer of 1943 destruction of Hamburg:

> The R. A. F., supported by the United States Eighth Army Air Force, flew a series of raids on Hamburg. The aim of Operation Gomorrah, as it was called, was to destroy the city and reduce it to ashes. Thousands of high-explosive and incendiary bombs were dropped on the densely populated residential area north

of the Elbe. A now familiar sequence of events occurred: first, all the doors and windows were torn from their frames and smashed by high-explosive bombs weighing four thousand pounds, then the attic floors of the buildings were ignited by lightweight incendiary mixtures, and, at the same time, fire bombs weighing as much as thirty pounds fell into the lower stories. Within a few minutes, huge fires were burning across the bombed area, which covered some eight square miles, and they merged so rapidly that, only a quarter of an hour after the first bombs had dropped, the whole airspace was a sea of flames as far as the eye could see. Five minutes later, at 1:20 a.m. a firestorm arose of an intensity that no one would ever before have thought possible. Reaching more than a mile into the sky, it snatched oxygen to itself so violently that the air currents reached hurricane force, resonating like mighty organs with all the stops pulled out at once. The fire burned like this for three hours. At its height, the storm lifted gables and roofs from buildings, flung rafters and entire advertising kiosks through the air, tore trees from the ground, and drove human beings before it like living torches. Behind collapsing facades, the flames shot up as high as houses, rolled like a tidal wave through the streets at a speed of more than ninety miles an hour, spun across open squares in strange rhythms, like spinning cylinders of fire. The water in some of the canals was ablaze. The glass in the tramcar windows melted; stocks of sugar boiled in the bakery cellars. Those who had fled from their air-raid shelters sank, in grotesque contortions, in the thick bubbles thrown up by melting asphalt. No one knows for certain how many lost their lives that night, or how many went mad before they died. When day broke, the summer dawn could not penetrate the leaden gloom above the city. The smoke had risen to a height of five miles, where it spread like a vast, anvil-shaped cumulonimbus cloud. A wavering heat, which the bomber pilots said they had felt through the sides of their planes, continued to rise from the smoking, glowing mounds of stone. Residential districts whose street length totaled a hundred and twenty miles were utterly destroyed. Horribly disfigured corpses lay everywhere. Bluish little phosphorus flames still flickered around many of them; others had been roasted brown or purple and reduced to a third of their normal size. They lay doubled up in pools of their own melted fat, which had sometimes already congealed. The central death zone was declared a no-go area in the next few days. When labor gangs of prisoners and camp inmates could begin clearing it, in August, after the rubble had cooled down, they found people still sitting at the tables where they had been overcome by carbon monoxide. Elsewhere, clumps of flesh and bone or whole heaps of bodies had cooked in the water gushing from bursting boilers. Other victims had been so badly charred and reduced to ashes by the heat, which had risen to a thousand degrees or more, that the remains of families consisting of several people could be carried away in a single laundry basket.

Churchill wrote to Lord Beaverbrook that "there was only one way to force Hitler back to confrontation, and that is an absolutely devastating exterminating attack by heavy bombers from this country upon the Nazi homeland." The idea to annihilate the civilian population of Germany was not just to bring the war to a swift conclusion, but it was thought to be the only way to win.

All the able-bodied could do was to try to help those in more desperate need. Mother said she didn't remember how long she wandered the streets, but she could not tell night from day. As the billowing flames shrunk into the rubble heaps and turned to smolder all across the city, some order was restored by the government, and aid stations were set up to move the homeless out of Hamburg and into the country. No one asked questions; authorities directed all the ambulatory survivors to a train and told them where to get off and which family they would be staying with. The *New Yorker*'s Sebald article describes that "the exodus of survivors from Hamburg had begun on the night of the air raid itself." It started, as Hans Erich Nossack writes in *The End*, with "constant movement in all the neighboring streets . . . going no one knew where." The refugees, numbering more than a million, dispersed all over the Reich as far as its outer borders. The diarist Friedrich Reck, under his entry for August 20, 1943, describes a group of some forty or fifty such refugees trying to force their way into a train at a station in upper Bavaria. As they do so, a cardboard suitcase "falls on the platform, bursts open and spills its contents. Toys, a manicure case, singed underwear. And last of all, the roasted corpse of a child, shrunk like a mummy, which its half-deranged mother has been carrying about with her, the relic of a past that was still intact a few days ago."

Mother also boarded the train in her torn evening pajamas and burned house shoes, not knowing where she was heading; she sat next to a worn-looking woman who appeared comatose and was gazing out the train window without seeing anything. Mother asked her about her home. She said, "My husband and my only children, three sons, all were killed in the war. Now my home is gone."

In his famous letter, Abraham Lincoln consoles Mrs. Lydia Bixby, a mother of five sons who were thought to have died in the American Civil War, that her sons "died gloriously on the field of battle." He writes of the "solemn pride that must be yours to have laid so costly a sacrifice upon the altar of freedom." Did this lady's sons die gloriously? I wonder if she was proud. Is any death glorious? Does that mean war is glorious? How many Mrs. Bixbys does a war make? There was no one to write this bereaved parent a letter, thanking her for her human sacrifices. Mother said to her, "What are you going to do?" She looked at Mother as if to say what kind of strange question is that! She answered, "I'm going to start all over. What else can I do?" Mother never forgot that. In her book, Murmurings, Mother reminisces:

> A person who has lost their nerve is a pitiful creature. They turn away from opportunity. But when they believe in themselves, they develop power and strength they did not know they had.

She decided she was pretty lucky. Although all the material possessions she had owned were destroyed, she still had her most prized assets: her health and that of her children. Mother said she had never met so many strong people. She noted that the women were more likely to keep their heads about them than the men. The train was crammed and overflowing with stunned, mannequin-like men, women, and children. The dull, unimpassioned human mass rocked quietly from side to side in rhythm with the clacking wheels of the train. Destination was unknown.

Area bombing, or bomb sweep, meant releasing all the bombs from an entire squadron in unison. Area bombing was sanctioned by the British government in February 1942 "to destroy the morale of the enemy civilian population and, in particular, of the industrial workers." But it didn't work. Sebald writes, "Critics of the bombing offensive also pointed out that, even in the spring of 1944, it was emerging that, despite incessant air raids, the morale of the German population was unbroken, while industrial production was impaired only marginally at best, and the end of the war had not come a day closer." Neither was Mother's spirit broken. She emerged stronger than ever. Enlightenment follows horror when you realize that you're alive, have all your body parts, can still breathe on your own, and your loved ones are safe. Mother constantly thanked God for sparing all the things in her life that were precious to her: her children and her health. Klaus and I grew up with the same appreciation. We enjoy beauty and appreciate quality, but we keep all material possessions in proper perspective to the meaning of life. Many of Mother's friends teasingly insisted she was really German because she was so strong. But Mother said it was her faith in God and her loving family environment in Barbour County, Alabama, that laid the foundation for her courageous resolve to push forward and not look back or pine for what has vanished forever. Our home had been in an area that had few survivors, and our three names were listed among those counted as deceased or missing. The mere fact that all three of us were alive and unscathed was blessing enough. It would be a sin to weep.

The train stopped in Warstade by Stade, about fifty miles west of Hamburg, to let Mother and a few other survivors off. Basically, I think it was just a train stop with a sparse scattering of off-the-dirt-road farmhouses in the fields. I guess it's hard for most comfortable home owners to realize how simple it is for authorities to knock on the door and direct you to take in a misplaced family. That's it. There is nothing you can do or say but okay. That's how we were assigned. Soon after the siege on Hamburg, Klaus and I received a telegram in Verden that Mother was all right and that she would contact us soon to let us know where she would be housed.

Klaus and I were put on the train to join Mother in Warstade. To the best of my recollection, it comprised mostly of one, wide, straight, unpaved road, lined with tall conifers and miles of grain fields surrounding humble farmhouses. The few tiny whitewashed homes lay like bird nests hidden in the wheat grasses. The dwelling of the family to whom we were assigned was no different. Family Guhr, a farmer, his wife, and children, were cordial, but it was plain to see that they were not happy about being forced to accommodate us. For that matter, they looked like they were never happy or had ever laughed. They remind me of Grant Wood's sister and a dentist posing with a pitchfork in his painting, *American Gothic*—long, lean, and tired.

We were steered to one room upstairs where all three of us slept. As I said, the house was neat, clean, mostly whitewashed inside and out. The front door opened into a combined kitchen and eating area. The house was ground level and the downstairs floors were cement. No rugs were evident. I don't recall a parlor, curtains or upholstered furniture. These rooms may have been in the house, but blocked-off. As with most families in Germany, only one room in the house or apartment was heated during the cold months. This was July/August, however, so we were quite comfortable. There was no school for us, and Klaus and I helped harvest wheat and feed the animals. I remember riding the hay wagon more than working. I think the farmer and his wife had two boys who were friendly and we all worked and lived together as one family. Mother took the train back into the city—center of Hamburg which was damaged but not destroyed by the bombardment. She said when she returned to Hamburg after the siege, she saw crews removing chunks of human remains from the rubble. The zoo, Hagenbeck, was severely damaged and burned during the bombing raids. Mother brought us sad and disturbing news about the trapped, terrified animals howling and screeching trying to clamber out of cages. The larger mammals broke loose in torment, dashing and pouncing through the streets, threatening and attacking nearby communities. News of the horrors and suffering of the aftermath spread quickly by murmured rumors, timorous behavior patterns, drawn facial expressions, and tired eyes still in shock. Mother pushed ahead in her new beginning with survival instincts refocused, determined to start over. On an irregular schedule, Mother traveled to her accountant job at Phris-Werke. Phrix-Werke informed Mother, by letter, that she should have returned to work by August 10, as announced in the newspaper, and will therefore only receive one half of her August salary. Mother was not able to return to work until four or five days later. Also, the letter persisted, that since she could not continue to live in Hamburg due to the danger to her children, she should therefore try to find employment elsewhere. Mother wrote the Burgermeister of Jesteburg requesting retroactive displacement compensation of 20 Reichmarks for herself and eight Reichmarks, each, for Klaus and me. She received a few clothes from the farm family and coworkers and was able to acquire and purchase other minor necessities. Mother reciprocated the Guhr's tolerance of us by bringing them specialty food items only available in the city. Our hosts had no money and no opportunity to purchase select foods such as honey, cheese, or sweets, and they were grateful to taste something besides the main war staples, black bread, potatoes, and cabbage. I think we were as interesting to them as they were dull to us. We all lived together harmoniously. There was no social interaction since we had little, other than survival, in common. The parents were stern but kind. They displayed little, if any, joy— either from too much work and responsibility or from lack of foreseeable future. Despite the war Klaus and I were not accustomed to living under such extreme peasant conditions and we felt oddly out of place. We never considered ourselves better, but the general ambience was too stark and basic according to our custom. An embroidered tablecloth on our table and eating from decorative porcelain with maybe some flowers on the table was the norm for us. Dreamy paintings hung on our walls and fresh curtains fluttered in the windows, but these people lived in another world. It was like watching black-and-white TV when you're accustomed to color. The spice was missing. There was nothing here to excite our curiosity or fulfill the possibility of a dream.

Sometime later, not too long after the bombing, we returned by train to Hamburg hoping to find the street where our home once stood. The entire civilian community of Hamburg looked like miles of salvage yard with heaps of rubble. The skeleton of a few multistory buildings remained erect. Their jagged brick structure created a field of giant sculptures silhouetted against a blank skyline. Ironically, many window—and doorframes were perfectly intact, like a five-story hollow decapitated dollhouse. All the beautiful trees were gone. Our eyes saw nothing but destruction. We were looking at a ghost town. Our neighborhood was quiet and void of life. A random scattering of young soldiers (or members of the Hitler Jugend) had been sparsely positioned on the abandoned rubble to prevent looting and to keep home-owners from endangering themselves while sifting through the ruins for what was their residence, in hopes of salvaging a bit of memorabilia. Mother, Klaus, and I found the heap where once stood the building of Parkallee Ten. We knew the street and the proximity of where our home once stood. As we climbed up the mountain of our collapsed apartment building, rummaging through debris like vagabonds on a city dump, we spotted something familiar. It was Klaus's baby cup (the one he didn't drop off the balcony) and a baby dish—the kind that one fills with hot water to keep the food warm—a perfectly intact demitasse cup, plus three other badly charred porcelain items. Most had generous clumps of hardened flows of molten phosphorus, and the metal dish was severely discolored and eroded. That's all we had time to find before one of the young soldiers asked us to come down because it was too dangerous. Mother said, "But this is our home." He apologized but insisted. Well, she started to cry as we reluctantly scrambled down. Then, of course, seeing our mother cry, Klaus and I started to cry, and then the young soldier was crying. He was so sweet. He kept saying he was sorry but insisted we must come down. We stood next to him, still crying. The four of us wept together as we faced our collapsed home and tried to grasp the significance this would have on our lives. Here, at our feet, lay a mountain of wreckage that represented our past and sheltered beautiful memories. The question that plagued Klaus and me was if our goldfish might have survived and if the two canaries could possibly have flown away. Mother said she didn't think the fish made it, but there might have been a small chance that the birds escaped. Honestly, I don't remember a single incident when I grieved over anything that was demolished by the bombing other than our living pets. That was a tremendous loss for Klaus and me. Their innocent death was hard to take. I always wanted to believe that the birds broke free. Mother tells of an incident where I saw something strange high in a burned tree. She said she recognized it as the head of one of my playmates, Maria.

The following official document, issued by the German police, was provided to Mother in March 1946 declaring that our home in

Hamburg Thirteen, Parkallee Ten, was struck to the ground on 25 July 1943:

TRANSLATION

93. Police district   Hamburg-Gross-Flottbek
                                                          16th March 1946

CERTIFICATE

This is to certify that the property (plot) located at Parkallee 10, Hamburg 13 was totally destroyed by an enemy air-raid on the 25th July 1943.

Mrs. Aurora R I T T E R suffered a total loss.

Signed:

Pfenningstop
Master of Police district

We rarely spoke or reminded one another of the total annihilation of all our material possessions. Klaus and I only hurt when we saw Mother tear-up. Periodically, something would trigger her memory, and for a few seconds, she'd get that distant look, and her eyes would well-up with tears. The loss of such items like our baby scrapbooks that she so meticulously and lovingly organized and maintained was particularly painful. Baby photographs, our handprints and footprints, bits of baby hair tied in a ribbon, our first words, plus various other details she wanted to preserve were lost forever. Mother had saved all of Klaus's drawings. He was exceptionally gifted in art at an early age and illustrated characters from stories Mother read to us. His picture of Siegfried, a heroic freedom fighter, won some acclaim. She would also sometimes mention the loss of her beautiful jewelry. "Onward Christian soldiers" was her motto. Be grateful for your healthy mind and body and move forward. In her *Murmurings*, she writes,

I began a diary in order to capture something worth remembering. Then came the war and the bombing of our

Hamburg, Germany, home in July, 1943, when all treasured keep-sakes were wiped out in one blast. Most prized of all were the memorabilia of my two young children. Both were childhood artists and as I read them favorite stories, they illustrated. Both children had huge folders, leather bound, especially made by hand just for their "prizes." And my own priceless china doll wearing an inlaid jewel necklace. She had been my silent companion each day of my life. The loss of these unredeemables will hurt forever—and forever.

Regret was short for Klaus and me. Life was exciting. Not necessarily in a positive way. We were never bored because some other adventure would soon come along to make us forget the past. Mother was a fighter and always ready for the next challenge. She constantly expressed gratitude for our health and for the fact that all three of us were spared any physical grief. Klaus and I were too young for that philosophy to register since it was obvious to us that all three of us would remain alive, well, and keep all our body parts in tact indefinitely. However, we were influenced by her optimism and knew that tomorrow would definitely be a better day. There was no time for self-pity. Mother never exchanged one minute of progress for a backward glance. None of the three of us has ever coveted or wished for material possessions in a serious way. Health, art, and education were what Mother preached. The first material gifts Mother bought for Klaus and me after the destruction were two original pieces of art. She bought an oil painting of a cottage in the woods for Klaus and a beautiful chalk drawing of a Persian cat for me—signed and dated in 1940. I have it on the wall of the room in which I write this. These are not masterpieces, but expressive and reminiscent.

GROSS-FLOTTBEK

"Ask anyone who has almost died and you'll find that they see life with a different perspective." A. E. Ritter, *Murmurings,* p. 88

WE RESIDED IN the Warstade countryside for what seemed only a few months before the German government reassigned us into one of Hamburg's suburbs, Gross-Flottbek. Gross-Flottbek was much closer to the center of Hamburg, making it easier for Mother to get to work by train. Our new temporary home was about four long blocks from the train station. It was the private home of Frau Wallman. Frau Wallman lived in a neat, two-story stucco house. The upper floor was more like a loft. The outer walls and wooden trim were painted yellow, but appeared to have faded to an antique manila with age. Our future home had several gables and was of an interesting architecture. The narrow, well planted and maintained front yard was fenced-off from the sidewalk. A slender footpath sliced the garden through the center and meandered to the back of the house. It was a friendly picture. Since Frau Wallman's home was quite large, she was ordered to accommodate several displaced single people as well as families. And as is common, she was also told which section of her home she should occupy. There was no choice in the matter. We never knew the folks upstairs since the three of us were assigned to two-and-a-half rooms on the main floor next to Frau Wallman. The lobby of her home was especially large for German standards (approximately twenty by twenty feet), and our rooms were directly off the main foyer. We had a fully furnished kitchen facing the front garden, the fence, sidewalk, and street. Our other room was originally the living/dining room, but served as our bedroom. It was situated at a right angle to the kitchen. The bathroom was in the hall. A huge armoire was placed against the sliding doors that separated us from Frau Wallman's quarters. The back of our "bedroom" was most likely the original dining room and the other side of the room must have been the sitting room. The sitting room area was one step up, like a small stage for a grand piano. It was rather charming and had an interesting curved bay window facing the front garden. This area was separated at the step by a heavy dark green drape. We often kept the drape drawn since it preserved our heat and gave us more privacy. I thought that it must have been beautiful when nicely furnished and decorated. There was a door between the kitchen and our sleeping area. Since we were devoid of any possessions, other than a few clothes, the space was ample and provided all the essential accoutrements for survival, plus a clean and cheerful ambience. We adapted easily to our new home; and the location was convenient to the train station for Mother, our new school, and to several little shops including a bakery and movie theater.

A word about Frau Wallman. After all, this was her beautiful home being invaded by all sorts of strangers. I'm not sure if we were required to pay rent. Anyway, Klaus and I called her Frau Wallepoops. She was at least in her late sixties or older. She was stout, short, and waddled slowly about her apartment, which no one ever entered. Klaus and I were enormously curious about Frau Wallman, so we crawled on top of the armoire, which came just to the bottom of the transom windows of the sliding doors separating our apartments. Once perched on the armoire, we had a perfect view of our neighbor's sitting area. (We never did this when Mother was home.) Her apartment, as far as we could see, was elegantly furnished and well kept. Her round tea table was directly on the other side of our separation. We had to be careful and quiet as we climbed on the armoire so she wouldn't hear us. Once on top, we had to lay flat since there was little crawl space between the top of the armoire and the ceiling. The surveillance was definitely worth our effort since we witnessed Frau Wallman talking to flies. Yes, she conversed with little flies that landed on her coffee cup or on her cakes as she enjoyed her regular afternoon kaffeeklatsch. All alone, she sat at her round antique coffee table on the same upholstered armchair facing a dainty tea service beautifully set on long lace or embroidered tablecloths and napkins. The table was set for two. Frequently, she wore gloves and hat for the ceremony. Without exception, we never saw Frau Wallman when she wasn't perfectly dressed as if she were being entertained at Buckingham Palace. Her conversations were credible, and her tone gave no hint that she was not communicating with *Homo sapiens*. These were two-way conversations since she answered for the flies. If one of the flies accidentally dove into her coffee, she'd quickly and tenderly extract it and release it to the outdoors. In a way, we felt sorry for her. I suppose she was lonesome, but she could have made friends with other residents.

Frau Wallman could be annoying in that whenever the sirens sounded for us to seek shelter, she was constantly the last person to toddle out of the house, which meant she would be the last to enter our dugout shelter and cork the exit. The house did not have a basement, but someone had dug an underground bunker in the backyard. This provided absolutely no protection against a direct hit from a bomb, but the dugout did safeguard us from shrapnel and being buried alive under our home. It was standard bunker conversation that each person would choose instant extermination in preference to injuries from toppling debris or death from slowly burning or suffocating. A dugout shelter such as ours was primitive. It looked exactly like a human-sized mole tunnel. It was generally ten to twelve feet long, barely four feet wide, and maybe forty-six inches high. The underground depth was roughly three feet. The rest of the height was aboveground and mounded up with dirt. Each side of the dugout shelter had a narrow, wooden plank built on each side against the dirt walls. Our knees touched as we huddled across from one another. The first person to arrive had to go all the way to the back of the dugout and consequently be the last person out. There were no lights. At night everyone had to carry his own flashlight. The entrance was secured with a simple wooden door. Well, on one particular occasion, in the middle of the day, when Klaus and I were home alone, the air-raid alarm sounded, and we headed for the dugout shelter. Like most war seasoned individuals, Klaus and I were also slow to get out of the house since we didn't like the idea of being stuck in the back of the dugout. Besides feeling claustrophobic, getting trapped was another fear. Of course, this defied all logic. In such a small, covered foxhole-type shelter, it's all or nothing. Either you make it or you don't. Anyway, I was walking through the entry hall just as Frau Wallman, who, as I mentioned, was notoriously late, stepped out her apartment door. She had an umbrella with her, and as we reached the front entrance of the house together to step outside, she opened her umbrella. It was a beautiful, sunny, clear day. I was puzzled. She hesitated a bit and analyzed the sky as she stood there holding the umbrella over her head. I also stopped and looked up to see what she was studying. I saw a pure blue sky and heard no planes. She gave an elegant appearance in a frilly yellow dress, purse, and parasol. I asked her why she had the umbrella. She was a kind lady and sweetly explained to me that she holds it over her head to protect her from bombs and shrapnel if a bomb should explode nearby. She was so sincere. I was stunned and utterly lost for words, so I just ran around the house to the backyard and squirmed into the shelter. The grown-ups in the shelter were already irritated with Frau Wallman for always coming last and plugging the entrance with her plump body. Not only was she stout but she was also slow. Frau Wallman was somewhat sad, but she was gentle, and I liked that in her. Mother said we'd be a bit weird too if all these strangers came and took over our house. I think she had problems long before that, but no one ever displayed open hostility toward others. We all were survivors. Confrontation saps too much energy when you're trying to stay warm, feed yourself, and dodge bombs. War fixates one's priorities on survival, not on petty disagreements.

Klaus and I were registered into a new school about six or seven blocks from home. However, because of the constant interruptions by siren warnings of air raids, we had much more free time than confinement to our classroom. The school system provided hot lunches when possible, and it was expected that each morsel must be eaten since there was a shortage of healthy foods. Most days we would have beets, cabbage, rutabagas, and potatoes; and the other days we had soup made of potatoes, rutabagas, cabbage, and beets. Our school lunches could be as stressful as the bombings. As I mentioned before, Klaus did not care for meat and especially fatty parts. The soup invariably had microscopic bits of Speck (bacon fat) floating in it. Klaus has always been creative. When no one was looking, he would put a piece of Speck on the nail of his middle finger and, with his thumb, flicked the Speck hard enough to hit the ceiling and stick. He did this one piece at a time. Klaus thought he had found the solution to ridding his soup of Speck, and for quite some time it worked. However, all good things must come to an end, and it wasn't long before some little boy sitting at his table ratted on him. When the teacher looked up, there they were on the ceiling— dozens of little dried flecks of bacon fat stuck overhead, like tiny, shining, gray pearls. The teacher was upset and lectured Klaus on how expensive and rare it was to have meat and how fortunate we all were to have bacon fat included in our food. She expressed dissatisfaction to Mother. Mother took a lighter view of the folly. For me, it was a bit more difficult to hide my beets. I simply could not eat beets. They tasted like dirt. I ate almost everything except meat fat and beets. We always ate at our desks. Our desks were actually tables. Whenever beets were served, I shoved my beets on a piece of paper and put them in my desk drawer. After several weeks, the teacher saw that my table drawer was full of dehydrated beets. She couldn't believe her eyes. She was stern with me and scolded me severely. Again, I received the lecture about food shortages, and the importance of the nutrition in beets. I wasn't so much concerned about her scolding as I was to find an alternative solution to disposing of my beets. What should I do? I panicked since I literally could not eat beets without gagging. The beets were always served sliced and as a hot vegetable. Finally, I conceived the idea to slip them in my satchel or coat pocket. We often wore our overcoats in class while we did our studies. Mother was not happy about the red stain in my coat pockets. Discipline, perfection, and good manners were expected by our teachers. Also, I was reprimanded while I was in a bathroom stall. I heard my name being called and replied with the word "was" (what) instead of "yes" or "wie bitte [how, please]." I didn't know I was responding to a teacher. Anyway, the teacher was upset with me and said that I had been told over and over again not to respond with "what" when someone calls my name. It was considered a highly rude and impolite reply to an adult. She made me a lifetime conformer.

Gross-Flottbek was a clean, well-planned town. The streets were broad and the houses and gardens were well maintained and clean. Most private homes had small english gardens in front—little grass, mostly flowers, herbs, and shrubs. The larger trees were usually along the street because the Germans love sunshine and too many tall trees around the house block the coveted sun. Trees in the yard were mostly fruit trees. Klaus and I enjoyed the abundance and variety of flowers as we walked home from school. The temptation to reach our hands through the fence along the sidewalk and pluck flowers was just too great and by the time we reached home, we had a nice little mixed bouquet to present to Mother. We wanted to be fair, so we never took more than one or two flowers from a single garden.

On one occasion, when Klaus and I were walking home from school we found a little bat. He looked quite young and ill. We brought him home and fashioned a cozy house out of a tin can. We turned the can so it was horizontal and wired it to a tree in front of our kitchen window. We filled the can with torn bits of dry grass and paper, placed the bat inside and fed him bugs. In a couple of days he was dead.

The only time I can recall Mother ever really loosing her temper with Klaus and me was at Frau Wallman's. We were having supper. Each of us was rationed one hot dog. Although Klaus and I were not big meat eaters, we loved hot dogs. I eagerly ate all of mine right away, but Klaus saved his to eat last. Near the end of our meal, Klaus took his hot dog and reached across the table and wagged it into my face saying: "See, I still have mine and you don't. Ha-ha." On reflex, I thrust my head forward and bit off half his hot dog. Klaus was stunned. So was I actually. I couldn't give it back to him, of course, so I swallowed it. Well, a major scrap ensued. Loud accusations were exchanged across the table. Mother couldn't settle us down. So she said she was going out in the yard and find a switch. This stopped us, because she had never hit us before. She marched out the door and around to the front yard and searched for just the right size of stick. Klaus and I ran to the kitchen window and watched her select a branch. She came back into the kitchen and raised the stick. Klaus and I ran around to the opposite side of the table. Mother chased us around the table. The three of us were chasing around and around the kitchen table. Finally, Klaus and I started giggling until Mother couldn't contain her anger any longer, and the three of us went into hysterics, laughing so hard that we were crying. Mother never could stay angry with us. She was totally incapable of being mean or vengeful.

Even though our few rooms at Frau Wallman's were sparsely furnished and humble, Mother quickly replaced many of our books. Reading was an evening ritual we couldn't live without. We spent many nights laughing and crying together as Mother sat on the side of our bed and read short stories, poems, and books to us. I must list some of our favorite children's books here. They are still in our home today:

1. *Der Struwwelpeter* by Dr. Heinrich Hoffman. This thin hard-page book has seven or eight children's stories told in rhyme. The verses and highly colorful illustrations reflect typical children's "misbehaviors."
2. *Der Zitronenritter* (*The Lemon Knight*) by Von Anne Kayssler-Beblo. This is a fascinating fairy tale about fruits and vegetables all characterized as people.
3. *Brüder Grimm, Kinder und Haus Marechen,* a large book of fairy tales by Jakob and Wilhelm Grimm
4. *Robinson Crusoe* by Daniel Defoe
5. *Wilhelm Bush Album,* four hundred pages of delightful verses and sketches of Max and Moritz (two mischievous boys)
6. *Molli* by Clare Newberry and translated from English to German. This is a story about a little boy and Molli, his kitten. Oma gave this to Klaus in 1944.
7. *Wuhs Wundersame Wanderung* by Anton van de Velde. This is a precious story about a family of owls, the Wuhs.
8. *Klein Erna, Ganz dumme Hamburger Geschichten* (*Littlel Erna: stupid Hamburg Stories*) by Vera Möller. Klein Erna was a stupid young girl. In one episode, she asked her boyfriend if he wanted to see where she had her appendix removed, and he eagerly replies, "Oh yes!" Then she points to the hospital across the rail.

Although some children's stories like these in *Struwwelpeter, Brüder Grimm,* and *Wilhelm Bush Album* had violent and crazy consequences, it was apparent to any school-age child that these were fun-fictions. Reading, playing table games, and drawing were typical ways we spent our evenings and many days during the long, gloomy winters.

Besides good books, my cultural, and sometimes sexual, education was supplemented by our young neighbor playmates. They had ditties for everything. We chanted rhymes about famous people such like Germany's outstanding poet, Johann Wolfgang von Göthe (1749-1832), and his close and influential friend, the poet and dramatist who wrote the legend of William Tell, Friedrich von Schiller (1759-1805). My new playmates in Gross-Flottbek were amazingly well informed. They also taught me dirty ditties about how babies are made and homosexual behavior. All this information on a sunny afternoon in our side yard. I didn't discuss the latter with Mother for fear my education would come to an abrupt halt, but I wondered about such inconceivable behaviors. I cataloged each detail in the confidential files of my memory for later reference.

We, along with most German children, found interest in collecting bomb shrapnel. When a bomb explodes, the steel casing is ripped apart into thousands of various sizes of razor-sharp jagged fragments. Also, the inside of a bomb may have shrapnel balls that explode in flight by a time fuse. The bomb debris scattered for hundreds of yards into the neighborhood. The shrapnel we collected was from five to six inches to splinter size. The larger the shrapnel, the more "valuable" it was to us children. One piece of shrapnel could have dozens of pikes that protruded like serrated knife tips and cut like broken glass. After one particular daytime air raid, we were in our dugout shelter behind the house when the bombs whistled so close that the explosion seemed louder than usual, and the ground quaked uncomfortably. We knew we had barely escaped death and that the hit was within a couple of houses from us. After the all-clear signal, the neighbors in the community came out of their shelters and hurried toward the area where the bomb hit. As luck had it on this day, the bomb sailed directly into someone's backyard and didn't break a brick; just some windows were blown-out, and a few trees were down. It was an awesome sight. I guessed the center of the crater to be slightly deeper than a one-story building. The displaced fresh soil created an earthen berm around the hole and pitched across the neighboring backyards. We all just stood and stared at this huge round hole which would have made a wonderful swimming pool. The explosion blasted a lot of virgin shrapnel into the neighborhood and we didn't waste any time searching around for our share. Some of the larger pieces had numbers stamped on them, or were painted in various colors, or were of an unusual shape and texture. These were considered real treasures. We children traded shrapnel like kids today trade baseball cards. We kept our collection on top of a cabinet in the kitchen.

The time was late 1943 to early 1944 and air raids occurred predictably, day and night. Siren warnings came incessantly. Sometimes two or three times a day. Usually the planes flew past, but our day was interrupted. Some evenings or days we had several attacks or waves of bomber squadron over flights. We still went to school because we seldom had bomb attacks in the early mornings and Gross—Flottbek, like most of Hamburg's suburbs, was not generally targeted for bombardment. If the sirens gave us enough warning while we were at home, the three of us sought shelter at the neighborhood high school. The college preparatory school was a little more than two long blocks from our home. The building had a large basement that was well fortified and stocked with cots and other necessities. It was definitely preferable to the dugout behind Frau Wallman's house. One peaceful, full-moon night, around 11:00 p.m., after my bedtime, the siren sounded and Mother dressed me and we ran toward the high school. Klaus was in the hospital near Hamburg. I think he had a broken arm. About halfway to the school, Mother and I saw the sky light up with dozens of "Christmas trees" dropped by the enemy to illuminate ground targets. It was like the Fourth of July fireworks at the Washington Mall. An air war against a midnight sky is a thrill that you hate to love. It encompasses the full range of feelings and emotions that make us human. German searchlights were crisscrossing the sky and we could already hear the humming of planes approaching. The artificial light cast an eerie blue look on us and everything about us as far as we could see. It was fear inspiring and I was scared. We had no time to get to the school shelter and dashed into the nearest private house. We walked to the back of the house and saw a thin streak of light under the basement door. Mother knocked on the door and we were let in. No one thought anything of our intrusion. Mother knew the owners. They said, "Oh, Mrs. Ritter, we're so glad you are here, we feel protected when you are with us." I guess they figured the enemy wouldn't kill one of their own. Mother was usually calm, since she was convinced that her mother was protecting us. She also felt confident that our lives would be spared. Even strangers said that Mother released a certain energy that made them feel relaxed and more secure. This house also had several displaced bombing victims assigned to live with the owners. It was a severely frightening night, with hours of persistent thunderous booms from cannons and bombs. People never speak in shelters because they're too focused on analyzing the war sound. Then when the final cracking bang comes, our downcast eyes look up again and we look at each other as if to say "we're still here." Mother's concern this night was Klaus's safety since the bombardment clearly incorporated Hamburg and suburbs. We could see the search lights over the city. She held me close. When the all-clear sounded we went home and I went to sleep immediately. Mother tried to call the hospital. I don't think she was able to reach anyone until the next day. She was frantic since many of the communication lines were damaged. Finally, she got through and was able to speak with Klaus. He was exuberant and excited and described to Mother in detail how interesting all the buildings and streets looked in the light of battle. He was on the top floor of the hospital and had a wonderful panoramic view of a city under siege. The nurses had to pry him away from the window and ordered him to go to the basement.

Gross-Flottbek had a couple of movie theaters. Censored films for children are usually shown on Saturday afternoons. The ticket line was always long. Gross-Flottbek wasn't like Hamburg, before it was razed, where we could have our choice of interesting places to visit. Actually, I don't remember ever going to a movie in Hamburg. Films, of course, were in black and white and always carefully censored for children. I remember once the theater featured a Sonja Hennie movie. Sonja Hennie was the popular Norwegian ice skater during the 1930s. Although this was strictly a film about ice skating, children were not permitted in the theater. I couldn't quite understand why ice skating scenes were bad for children to watch, so naturally, one tries to imagine what naughty things might be showing on the screen. The most risqué thought that came to my mind was that Sonja probably was skating in a short skirt and had to kick her legs so high that her knickers were exposed. Each time I passed the theater on my way back and forth to school, I turned my head to study the poster on the theater marquee where Sonja was posing and I wondered again what I was missing.

Gross-Flottbek, like all European towns, had a wonderful bakery. Sugar was scarce during the war, so sweet pastries were limited in variety and supply. Bread in every shape, grain, and color-white or dark-was available. The Gross-Flottbek bakery made the most delicious *Brötchen* (small hard-crusted breads). They were about the size and shape of a goose egg and tasted much like French bread: soft inside and crisp outside. Klaus and I would poke a hole in the top and dig the soft dough out with one finger until the Brötchen was almost hollow. Then, we'd put sugar and milk or butter in the center and pretend it was gourmet pastry. Germans use sugar beets to produce their sucrose instead of sugar cane. Since the whole beet was nutritious and easy to grow, it was used primarily as a vegetable staple. Consequently, the table sugar was heavily rationed, and our monthly ration cards were never enough to satisfy our cravings for sweets.

We lived with Frau Wallman about three quarters of a year before the German housing authorities reassigned us to live with another family that was more suitable to children. No one ever asked questions. I really don't know if Mother had any input to the location of our various dwellings, but none of us was particularly perturbed by the transfer. We simply learned to deal with change and accepted our destiny without protest. We were assigned to a single-family house owned and occupied by a war widow and her four children. Our new home was also in Gross-Flottbek, about five blocks away on the opposite side of town. The distance to the train station was a bit closer to our new location. Trains were the only mode of transportation, and the station's proximity was always a major consideration so Mother could go to work. Our new section of town was called Ottmarschen. Frau Lemke was our new landlady. Her home was located on Rosenhagenstrasse Three. Her husband had been killed about nine months before we arrived. With four children ranging in ages from six to thirteen, she was not able to work and take care of her brood. Mother, in effect, became the breadwinner for all eight of us since she was employed. Mother turned all our ration cards over to Frau Lemke. This included her cigarette cards, which were highly prized as legal tender. There was no law against swapping ration cards, and although Mother used to enjoy about one cigarette a month, now she traded her cigarette cards for sugar cards. Frau Lemke was the homemaker and took care of the cleaning, cooking, laundry, gardening, and anything else required to care for the five of them plus Mother, Klaus, and me.

Mother and Frau Lemke became cordial friends. She came from an educated background. Her late father was a judge. Her mother was still living and on occasion invited all of us for tea. Frau Lemke was formal. She had almost no sense of humor, which, I expect, was the result of too much worry and responsibility. She and Mother had hard work, survival, and integrity in common, but differed in personality and political views. Nevertheless, they respected each other. The children's names in descending order were Inge, Ursula, Anette, and Juergen—three girls and one boy. Ursula was the only one of our age—nine or ten. We blended rather well, but we also lost our independence. We had never had to spend every waking moment with "strangers." Merging two cultures into one family was not easy for anyone—children or adults. Maybe Mother preferred it this way so she didn't have to worry about us being home alone so much when air raids forced schools to close at all hours of the day. Klaus and I missed our freedom and missed not having Mother to ourselves, but it was good not to come home to an empty house. Frau Lemke was a large-boned woman in her forties, attractive, and proud, with a caring quality about her. She was a good organizer and managed Mother's money and us with dependability and honesty. It was a business for her, and she was a good businesswoman.

The house had two levels with three or four bedrooms and one full bathroom upstairs. Facing the backyard, the ground floor had a galley kitchen and a dining room. In the front of the house, facing the street, were the sitting room and a living room with a walkout balcony. The entire house was off-limits to us except the kitchen, sitting room, bathroom, and our assigned upstairs bedroom, where all three of us slept. This rule applied also to her children. There were two reasons for this. One reason was that only one room in the house had heat in it, and the other reason was that Frau Lemke didn't want to clean the entire house. Christmas, Easter, and a few other special occasions were the exceptions for using the living room. We never used the dining room. When it was cold, which was most of the time, only the sitting room was heated by a black iron coal-burning stove in the corner. All the other rooms in the house were icy—including the bathroom. We layered our clothes to keep warm and heated bricks on the potbellied stove to take to bed with us to warm our feet. Besides the stove, the sitting room barely had space enough for a conference-sized table in the middle, with sufficient chairs around it to accommodate all of us. We literally LIVED in this room during the day. We ate, did our homework, played games, talked, and practiced music—Klaus, Inge, and Ursula took flute lessons—all in this one room. But it was always heated and that was worth the close companionship. I began piano lessons while we lived on Rosenhagen Street. My music teacher lived directly next door—behind the herb garden. She was a talented young lady who also was an accomplished artist. Mother commissioned her to paint a portrait of me in water color which hangs in my home. I had to practice the piano at my teacher's house since Frau Lemke didn't own a piano.

On warm summer days we enjoyed the yard and the porch, and the flute players were allowed to practice in the living room. Frau Lemke helped me with my knitting and treated us like her own children—with a few exceptions. One obvious exception was our breakfast. As mentioned before, our breakfast always consisted of hot oatmeal or cream of wheat. Frau Lemke invariably cooked two batches: one with milk and one with mostly water. Klaus and I were always served the watered-down version. You could tell by the color of the oatmeal or farina who was served the whiter porridge. Also, she allowed her children more time to hug the stove to warm up. We took turns standing by the iron stove. The rule was whoever came in from the outside—like when we came home from school—automatically received preference closest to the stove, and whenever someone else came in, the warm person had to move over and let the cold person thaw. Sometimes Frau Lemke listened to her children when they told her that their turn in front of the stove wasn't long enough. In which case Klaus or I were cut short on our warm-up allowance. I found this very annoying. Thawing was an important event that we coveted. Challenging an adult was not tolerated and we never made issues of these situations. With eight people living in such close quarters, it was imperative that peace be kept. We had to live in harmony and we did. No one ever fought. In spring all of us had to participate in weeding the vegetable and herb garden. In the summer we harvested strawberries, picked cherries, shelled peas, and pulled strings off beans and snapped them. Fall was the time to collect apples and pears from the backyard trees and dump them down the chute into the basement where they stayed cool and fresh throughout most of the year. In winter we froze. Christmas was the only day we moved about in two warm rooms. Frau Lemke splurged on Christmas, and the living room where the tree stood was heated, plus of course, the candles gave off more warmth. All evening meals were formal, and we children could not sit until Frau Lemke sat. After dinner we would ask to be excused, walk to the head of the table where Frau Lemke sat, extend our hand and thank her for a good meal. Her girls and I would make a *Knicks* (curtsey) and Klaus and her son would make a slight bow. It taught us humility, gratitude, and respect for all her hard work. Klaus and I were always expected to bow and curtsey when we were introduced to adults. I did not find such manners objectionable as a child.

After completing our evening meal and homework, we'd each heat our brick on the iron stove, wrap it in a towel, and hug it tight until we went to our bed upstairs. In winter that's all you could do— go to bed once you left the only heated room in the house. We took our weekly bath in a large unheated bathroom. Just a rationed amount of water was heated for the special bathing event. Our bedroom consisted of two three-quarter size beds, a sink complete with flowing ice water, two chairs and a small closet. Mother alternated sleeping with Klaus and me. This arrangement was always systematically planned since each of us wanted an equal share of her attention and warmth. Although we had fluffy down covers under and on top of us the thawing process took awhile before we were able to generate enough body heat to warm the sheets. Also, we had become creative in dressing and undressing under the covers. I had already gone to sleep one evening when I was awakened by something scratching on my head. I wasn't about to take my hand from under the warm covers and check what was going on up there, so I called to Mother, who was sleeping with Klaus. Just as she raised her head to look at me, a little mouse ran along the side of my ear, down along the cover, across my feather bed, and jumped to the floor. We heard him scamper across the room. Then we heard something rearrange our shoes. Mother said the poor little mouse was cold too and was just trying to find a warm place to sleep in our shoes. I certainly could relate to that and took no issue as long as it wasn't my hair he was making into his bed.

It's amazing we learned anything in school between 1943 and 1945. I firmly believe that any progress made during that time was from our homework—which was always checked and graded by the teacher. If we actually went into the classroom, the sessions were short, and the school was not always heated. Even when we only lined up in a single-file row in front of our teacher, she would merely do a roll call, collect homework, return graded papers, and distribute new assignments. Parents did most of the teaching. I guess one might say all German school-age children living in the cities were mostly home schooled. Teachers set the standards and corrected our papers; but parents, older siblings, or anyone in the household provided explanations, taught us how to read, checked our math, listened to us recite our multiplication tables, and made sure our penmanship was flawless. All graded assignments had to be signed by an adult and returned. This also applied to many of our art projects.

It was near the end of the war. We still had not heard any news of Vati's whereabouts or even if he was alive. It had been months. Klaus and I always asked Oma or Annenie if they had heard anything from Vati, but they never changed their story. It was always the same. He was missing. Klaus and I suspected they knew much more than we were told, but for whatever reason, they thought it best we did not know.

Frau Wallman's home. We occupied the two downstairs rooms

Frau Lemke and children

Mother and Frau Lemke

THE LAST SHOT

*Accept if you want to stay sane? I lay awake
pitting logic against emotion.* A. E. Ritter, *Murmurings,* p. 16

TOWARD THE END of the war trains were not necessarily a dependable mode of transportation, and there was no guarantee that you would arrive at your destination on time, if at all. Frequently, the trains ran out of coal midway between stations; and all the passengers gathered their luggage, got off the train, and started hiking the rest of the way. Most of the trains looked like old boxcars. Sometimes they were so full we had to sit on bleachers built along the side of cattle cars. On one particular journey I remember an old woman all bundled up sitting directly across from me. Her black shawl covered her head and upper body. She wore a long black coat over a black skirt. Her legs were kept warm with thick brown hose that were all crumpled up. She wore well-darned heavy socks on top of her hose, and her black shoes looked like she had walked a thousand-mile marathon in them. After many years and many miles of walking in these old leather lace-up shoes, they had worn thin along the sides and molded to the shape of her feet. Sitting on bleachers in a box car with no windows one focuses across the isle and reads faces. The study is quiet and intense and the mind asks many questions. Who are you and where did you come from? Where are you going? Did you lose a family member in the war? Do you still have a home? Why do you look so worn? What possessions do you clutch in your bundle? Can you smile? They could not smile. Survival demanded all their energy. Their baggage was not in a suitcase but in their hearts. I wondered what they were thinking and what ordeal lay in their past and what was yet to come.

As another elderly peasant woman across from me fumbled around in her bags, she pulled out an egg. I thought she would peal it, but instead she poked a hole in the top of it with a knife and then held the egg to her mouth and sucked the contents. I was aghast. Then she repeated this maneuver with another egg. She reared her head back and made sucking noises as she inhaled the slick yolk and whites to make sure no nutrition was left in the shell. I probably shouldn't have fixated on her so intently. Mother elbowed me, and I recovered.

In late 1944 and early 1945, the fighting intensified so drastically that Mother wanted Klaus and me out of the Hamburg area. The end of the war was a foregone conclusion. Assassination attempts against Adolph Hitler had become almost routine when the majority of Germans, including his officers, realized that Hitler was mentally deranged. Most of the attempts were abandoned or Hitler was lucky and evaded the explosion with only slight injury. In 1944 when Adolph Hitler ordered Albert Speer, his most trusted Minister of Armament, to destroy Germany's facilities because he decided the Germans weren't worthy of his greatness, Speer concluded that Hitler had really gone mad and tried to gas him through a ventilation shaft that led into the bunker. However, the SS guards were too tight and the shaft was too exposed to approach without notice. Also, news that Admiral Canaris and his chief of staff were accused of participating in the anti-Hitler officer's plot on July 20, 1944 was rumored. Hitler dismissed Canaris from command in February and, later that year, placed him under house arrest, preventing him from participating in the plot. The Gestapo discovered evidence linking him to the conspiracy, and he was executed by hanging a few weeks before the end of the war. A similar fate befell Erwin Rommel. He came to realize that the war for Germany was hopelessly lost. After he was injured in a strafing attack, he was sent to the hospital and, from there, to his home under house arrest—despite the fact that there was no hard evidence linking him to a conspiracy to murder Hitler. When two agents were sent to his home to offer him a public trial (which would result in hanging) or death by suicide, he chose the latter. The German public was told that Rommel died of his injuries. Hitler gave an order for national mourning.

In March 1945, the three of us left Hamburg and boarded a train to Jesteburg to avoid the last resistance efforts by the Germans. It was about midafternoon when the train ran out of fuel and slowly glided to a full stop right in the middle of wheat fields. I guess it must have been at least ten miles or more from the Jesteburg station. The conductor walked alongside each railroad car and informed the passengers to get out and start walking to the next town, Jesteburg. Mother, Klaus, and I had two suitcases among us. We found a big stick and stuck it under the handle of each suitcase. Mother walked in the middle, holding a stick in each hand, and Klaus and I supported the outside of each stick. We walked along the tracks, on and on, into the night. Parts of the stretch had smooth country roads that paralleled the rails which we preferred for walking—rather than stepping over cross-ties and gravel. After we reached the train station, we turned to continue on familiar trail to the Unteutsch farm. About halfway between the station and our destination was a little bench, which was our landmark. Frequently, we'd stop there for a rest and snack before hiking on. I was so relieved to see our milestone. We didn't sit long since it was already midnight and getting cold. Finally, fully exhausted, with sore arms and feet and blisters on our hands, we reached the Unteutsch home. Sometime in the night and the next day, I had excruciating abdominal pains. All I could do was groan. Tante Martha brought me soup. Mother was worried that I had ruptured something. The doctor was summoned and declared, after a thorough exam, that I had overextended myself on the long hike and was suffering from extreme exhaustion. My body needed rest. I was allowed to lie on the living-room couch. I knew I must have been quite ill because no one was ever permitted to enter the living room except for special occasions. I recuperated within a week, but was cautioned not to lift anything heavy for a while.

We stayed with the Unteutsch family until June. In Jesteburg, news began reaching us that various border towns had already been captured by British and American ground troops. No German wanted to be caught in the Communist sector, and many residents of the eastern towns fled to the west. Many German soldiers, officers and enlisted, surrendered voluntarily to the British and Americans—eager for a final end to the fighting. The British were advancing toward Jesteburg. We heard rumors that all able-bodied persons were to fight to the end and that farmers put cook pots on their head, and use pitchforks to defend themselves and the Reich. I never saw such a thing. From what we gleaned, most Germans were glad the fighting was coming to an end.

We thrived on rumors. The gossip was exciting. Let's face it, war energized us and children love anything that breaks their routine. We'd wait for Erhard Unteutsch to come home from Hamburg to tell us what he'd heard. Mother added her version to the rumors from different sources. We learned of some looting but no assaults on individuals from either side. All in all, most Germans were relieved and willing to cooperate with the new authorities. We wondered what it would be like when the town of Jesteburg and surrounding farms were invaded by foreign soldiers. Would they hate us and hurt us? Would they set up a gendarme? Would they boss us around? Will someone come into your house and take what they want and tell you what to do in your own home? Could Onkel Erhard still go to work on the train? Will Mother still have a job? We would soon find out.

The first signs of foreign troops entering the town of Jesteburg came at midmorning. Of course, we were aware that the war was over for Germany, but no one knew what to expect next. All was quiet and there were no radio announcements. All of us on the farm were apprehensive and nervous. What would the enemy do to us? We knew something would change but we had gone so long without news that we could not imagine how the turnover of power would manifest itself. Around 10:00 a.m., we heard cannon fire in the distance. Adults and children ran out of the house and hurried through the woods to a high place on the edge of the forest where the clearing began just before the asparagus fields. This was a great vantage point to see the town of Jesteburg. Sure enough, we saw the first convoy of tanks roll slowly through the streets, one directly behind the other. There were no foot soldiers. We saw only one or two armed British soldiers sticking out of each tank hatch. The soldiers carried their rifles in the defensive position. German families were in front of their houses staring at the slow moving caravan, some waving, some just deadpan still. As the tanks thundered along the cobblestone road, some of the tanks raised their big guns and fired, straight over the heads of the onlookers, into the red terra cotta roofs of the houses lining the street—leaving black cavities the size of a head. Just one neat hole per house. Methodically executed. The soldiers didn't fire into each house, but enough to intimidate. I remember asking Mother why they were doing that. She said we shouldn't be afraid, that they were young men who were tired and all pent-up from fighting and that they were just releasing steam. I couldn't relate. I just took my mother's word for it.

We stood on the hillside and watched for a long time. It was a bit scary as we waited and wondered what would happen to us out here in the boondocks. We walked back to the farmhouse and continued our chores without focus or concentration since we were anxious regarding our destiny. We did not have to wait long. Early that same afternoon we heard the familiar thunder of a tank rolling in the distance. The sound was heading in our direction and thick dust clouds floated into the trees as the Panzer barreled toward us at top speed, louder and louder. Only the driveway of the farm is visible from the road. The farmhouse and garden are blocked by a thicket of conifers. We were relieved to see it hurtle past our driveway. Only one. We glimpsed the treads and part of the tank from the courtyard. We knew the tank had to return to town the same way it approached. Well, Mother decided this time was as good as any to make her acquaintance with the new English-speaking regime. She made up her mind that when the tank returned, she would intercept their path and introduce herself as an American so we could get on with our new life. She, with Klaus and me at her side, stood under the spruce trees close to the road, listening for the tank to reappear. Tante Martha and the others stayed in the farmyard well out of sight. As the tank bounced over a slight rise in the distant road on its return trip, Mother confidently stepped forward into sight directly into its path and held her hands up, waving for the troops to stop. A British soldier with a rifle aimed at us was standing in the hatch. Mother spoke in a self-assured, stentorian voice in clear English and said, "I am an American. I want to see an officer!" The soldier took aim and shot right over Mother's head and screamed, "You're a goddamned liar!" Now Mother turned angry—shots or not. Those were fighting words down South. No one ever, I mean ever, called a lady a damned liar. Mother hollered to Klaus and me to get back. We bolted. She never moved. She just repeated her statement that she was an American citizen and wanted to speak to an officer. The Brit took aim again and barked some more cuss words. We could hear Mother say a few other things to him, and then they rumbled off. We thought that was the end. I know Mother's heart was beating fast, but she's just like a stone once she makes up her mind. The soldier would have had to shoot her if he wanted to see her move. The shot didn't frighten Mother. It was the fact that someone dared to call her a goddamned liar that infuriated her to eruption. She was absolutely incensed and mumbled about the audacity of such an insult as she came back up the path with fire in her eyes.

Late afternoon that same day, we heard a motorcycle struggling to maneuver up the curved and rugged driveway toward the house. We walked to the front door as the rider approached. He stopped his cycle directly parallel to the front door and balanced his bike with his left boot on the first step where Mother and Tante Martha were standing. We children peeked out from behind the adults. There was only one rider. We had never seen a foreigner, the enemy, up close before. I thought he was brave and ever so handsome in his crisp uniform and high leather boots. He explained that one of his men had informed him that an American was living at this address who wanted to speak to an officer. Mother finally had her officer— even if he was British. He removed his hat when he spoke to Mother but remained seated on the cycle. I saw a pistol in his holster. The gentleman was extremely courteous and amazingly pleasant looking to be the enemy. He and Mother talked business while Klaus and I and all the rest of the household never took our eyes off the foreigner. He looked so normal. All our personal papers such as passports, citizenship, baptismal, and medical records had been burned when our home was destroyed; and Mother was eager to reestablish herself within the new government. Tante Martha slipped back into the house. She returned a few minutes later balancing a glass of milk, literally filled to the brim, in her hand. A generous offer, I might add. She moved in front of Mother and offered the milk to the officer. He politely declined, and Tante Martha drank the entire glass of milk directly in front of him until it was empty. I was standing next to her and looked up as she proceeded to drink all the milk, every drop, tipping her head so far back I thought she would lose her balance. I was embarrassed to death. I didn't think that was a mannerly thing to do in front of any stranger. After the officer left, I couldn't wait to ask her why she had done that. She explained she didn't want the gentleman to think the milk was poisoned, so she indicated her sincerity by drinking it all herself.

POSTWAR GERMANY

The stone around and in my heart is not from lack of
feeling, but from feeling too much and from being completely
locked up in it. Everything is too heavy for me, heartbreakingly heavy.
NO self-pity. That I disclaim—and I know, I know. A. E. Ritter,
Murmurings, p. 58

GERMANY SURRENDERED UNCONDITIONALLY on May 8, 1945 (to Soviet forces on May 9). In February 1945, the three superpowers headed by Roosevelt, Churchill, and Stalin (later joined by France) partitioned Germany and Austria so that most of Eastern Europe came under Soviet control. Borders among the four countries, including France, were identified and implemented immediately throughout Germany. The American, British, Russian, and French zones were defined by road barriers, fences, dogs, and men. A mass exodus began from districts rumored to possibly be included in the Soviet zone. Neither the Soviets nor Communism were popular with the Germans, and contrary to the other three countries, Stalin, like Hitler, was considered a dishonest barbarian who manipulated and controlled the Russian empire with tyranny. All the propaganda we heard about the Red Army terror proved to be true. When they entered Berlin, anything that was not destroyed was pilfered or smashed. Nearly all women old and young were raped. Drunken soldiers ransacked and looted the spoils with total disregard to history and art. Women even tried to dirty their faces or mark their bodies to claim disease to keep from being raped. One of Mother's best friends was raped repeatedly by three Russian solders in her Berlin apartment while her young daughter stood by screaming. Although my aunt and grandmother had not yet been directly affected by the "people's movement," restraining orders and controls were being posted, and the seizing and confiscation of private property had begun in their eastern border town of Verden. Hordes of families and soldiers from the eastern zone left everything in their homes and fled west on foot rather than risk the wrath of the Red Army. Soldiers caught escaping the Red Zone were shot. Again, out of Max Hastings' Armageddon:

> "Corporal Helmut Fromm, a sixteen-year-old soldier from Heidelberg, shared the agony of the encircled Ninth Army in the fields and forests south of Berlin after the city had fallen and Hitler was dead. In their thousands, some organized bodies and others alone, they trudged westwards, like some gigantic armed football crowd dispersing after a match, fighting Russians wherever they met them. The roads and surrounding countryside were jammed with fugitives, constantly attacked by Soviet aircraft. Sharing their misery were scores of thousands of civilian refugees of both sexes and all ages, clutching pitiful possessions."

Even British prisoners of war in German prison camps were starved and treated disrespectfully by their Soviet liberators. Although Verden was never occupied by Russia, rebellions of the laboring peasant class toward the educated wealthy emerged in Verden, and Oma and Annenie became afraid of riots and losing their home and personal possessions. They decided to leave their picturesque residence and garden on the Aller River in search for a safer domicile. In one of Mother's letters to her friend Hans (not my uncle), she writes, "The Lüneburger Heide, where we found refuge, was more or less the center of the front and afterwards the Poles and Russians were far worse than the enemy planes." Prisoners were released, and many turned their pent-up hate on innocent civilians. Rape, pillage, destruction, and other various assaults were terrorizing communities daily, especially towns near the Polish borders.

The following are two letters Mother wrote to friends after the war:

Hamburg/Germany
Othmarschen
Rosenhagenstrasse 3
(circa mid 1945)

My dear Emily:

Oh, yes, despite my hell of a life these past four years, you are still dear to me—to us all in fact. The children speak ever so frequently of you and remember in detail your unlimited kindnesses and thoughtfulness of us back in those dark days of '37 and '38. Are you still practicing being an angel, my dear? I'm not so sure that the dividends are worth while. Think about this before you break yourself for wicked humanity.

Are you still so active and growing more beautiful with the years? Are you a grandmother/ Has your interesting daughter married? Where are the boys? Did Allan have to serve in the army? These, and many more questions are flowing through my mind. Has Mr. Frojen's health improved? Your last letter was a "God send." It reached me in late 1941 just after war was declared with America and I was fighting like mad alone here in Hamburg to get a new start, a new home, furniture, position—and to regain the children in a court case that lasted for almost six months. *I WON!* Was it Solomon who said, "We increase our ratio of sorrow in comparison to knowledge"—in which event I should be getting quite wise. There is simply no end to the tragedy of the past 10 years but somehow I have a feeling now that the rainbow's end is just around the corner.

First of all I shall say, the 2 children and I came through the worst with healthy bodies and you don't have to remind me what a lucky thing that is. Literally, Emily, Germany is a WRECK! I presume that you have seen in the pictures the demolition of some of the cities. Hamburg's turn came in 1943. Within 3 to 4 bombing hours this city was not recognizable and some quarter of a million dead. My home—Parkallee 10—was caught by an Allied "block-buster" on the night of the 24-25th

July '43 and the home fell burning over our heads. With bodies torn, feet and hands burned we crawled out through a crevice and after hours and hours of fighting to live we slowly realized that we had saved nothing more than our naked lives. Literally for us and so many million more the YEAR I. When I think back now I cannot understand my own strength and courage. It all goes to say that the mind can control matter and that there is no end to human endurance if one has this Will to live on and on. I shall not attempt to go further into detail of the "European Tragedy." History will have a hard time getting it into a plastic picture for those who never heard the screeching of a siren nor the sizzzing of a bomb. ARMAGEDDON in every sense of the word—and that is putting it mild. It quite suffices me for life. May the world never have another war and even while writing this I believe that certain suspicions are cast toward Russia. Some 400 million people are under Russian jurisdiction today. Just give her sufficient time and her strength will be a warning to all other lands.

Since May we have changed our song from "Deutschland, Deutschland über Alles" To "God save the King" and it may interest you to know that your good old friend Aurora is in HIS MAJESTY'S SERVICE! Oh, what a world! This business of one country trying to run another is also a rotten job. I was the happiest soul on the continent as the English came in and they definitely have some excellent qualities. The reserve and conduct of the English soldier is indeed admirable but it is a frightful problem for them to get a tattered and torn country like this back into organized shape.

[Aurora]

Hamburg/Othmarschen
Rosenhagenstrasse 3
30 October 45

Dear Hans ! [a friend]

One never knows what happens from day to day in other parts of Europe, hence I was happily surprised to get your letter and therewith the news of your physical survival of the worst. Shall we congratulate ourselves for having come through the storm? After 6 months of apparent peace I am as yet unable to see the advantage offered. Life in this particular part of the world is far too strenuous, exerting and cold for one to call himself L U C K Y.

I left the city in March of this year in order to avoid the "close in" of the Allied against Hamburg, and by this move to get out of the excitement, we moved directly into it. The Lüneburger Heide where we found refuge was more or less the center of the front and afterwards the Poles etc. etc. were far worse than the enemy planes. But as you see, I came through and have begun slowly and surely my effort to find roots gain.

We returned to Hamburg toward the middle of June and I began immediately my move to get in with the British Military Government. Stated here, Esplanade 6, Administrative Detachment 609—on July 1st and haven't missed a day, nor an hour at my post since that time. This is saying quite a bit because we have unusually long hours, and the home responsibilities with children complicates my problem no little. The work here is more or less routine—nothing for the HEART—but WE have long since forgotten that particularly organ of the body. NICHT WHAR? Or am I supposing, Hans—you dear! I shall not attempt to go into any details about the past, present nor the uncertain future. Philosophizing doesn't help the solving of the tragedy. It seems certain that the whole matter of one country trying to run another is a rotten job. None of the Allies have made a rich inheritance.

I began immediately in June with efforts to get out of the country but to the present time I see no ship in sight and its more than my strength is equal to swim. I dislike to think of the winter months. We have no coal, no wood, limited gas and electric and for over 3 weeks not one potato in the cellar. Perhaps the rainbow's end lies just around the corner. It cheers one up to think so! At any rate the British manner of conduct and his composure is admirable. I have absolute confidence that within the next hundred years we shall have Bohnenkaffee [fresh ground coffee] and tea with sugar again. *Also, sei froh!* [So be happy!]

I have 2 small rooms out in Othmarschen now, 7 minutes walk from Klaus Groth 39. We live with a young war widow that has 4 children of her own and takes care of my 2 orphans during my absence. Lt. Col. Ritter was held in Neugamme [Neuengamme Prison] the last we heard of him. Have heard no further details and am frankly not interested.

Let me hear from you again and you might give me the American address of your sons. Perhaps I shall be able to give them a personal greeting from their dear old DAD one day before long.

Much love,
Aurora

As the troops continued their march into the Lüneburger Heide, Mother felt obliged to immediately go to Marxen. She realized that soon the search for war criminals and Nazi sympathizers by the British would identify Georg Mickel-Garbers's affiliation with the Nazi Party. She wanted to be there in case the Mickel-Garbers family was confronted. When we arrived in Marxen, the mood seemed in order. But rumors regarding the reorganization of local administrative networks were raging. Tante Herta and Onkel Georg were visibly uneasy and grateful and relieved that Mother had come. The grown-ups talked too much among themselves in low tones as nervous adults often do when expecting the unexpected. I couldn't quite understand why they appeared so upset. Several days after our arrival we heard the familiar rumble of a military convoy approaching. As we ran to the window we saw a motorcade of jeeps and covered military trucks pull into the Mickel-Garbers' courtyard. If one hasn't experienced confiscation of personal home and property it is difficult to comprehend how a total stranger can enter your house and claim it as theirs. However, that's just exactly what happened. A knock came on the door. Onkel Georg walked toward the front door—with household members directly behind him—jammed up close for a peak at the enemy. Three British officers presented themselves. Mother introduced herself as she stepped up to translate. The men asked if this was the home of Georg Mickel-Garbers, and of course, Mother said, "yes." The officers said, "We'd like to come in and look around." They had pistols strapped at the waist as they walked in. They were correct and mannerly but firm. They removed their hats and introduced themselves and in a matter of fact, but polite tone, said, "We've come to occupy your home. I need a place to stay for my officers and my troops." They wanted to see the layout of the house. Tante Herta and Mother showed them all the rooms. As they left they said to Herr and Frau Mickel-Garbers, "You can keep your bedroom, Mrs. Ritter and the children can sleep in the small room downstairs, and my officers and I will take the bedrooms upstairs, and the troops will sleep in your hay barn. I want the living room for my conference room. Also, I would like some of the meals served for my men and me in the living room." Onkel Georg and Tante Herta were solicitous and polite. No unkind or uncivil words were exchanged. In fact, we all were relieved that the officers had not come to arrest Onkel Georg but had, instead, selected his property for their camp. His farm was by far the largest and most comfortable in the community. Of course, being children, we weren't really afraid for our lives. I think Klaus and I were mostly awestruck and excited, always wondering how the next change of events might alter our life. The British invaders were treated as royalty by all in the home. The adults saw to their smallest request with the greatest humility—realizing, of course, that it was the victors' prerogative to take anything in the home without asking. They took nothing and asked for nothing except food and bedding. The officers and enlisted were perfectly well mannered gentlemen and used the Mickel-Garbers home as their headquarters for that district. Onkel Georg was not arrested until later.

That's how things were after the war. We lived in harmony with the British troops in the home and yard. Mother, Klaus and I remained in Marxen for several weeks since there was no school. We children enjoyed the young British enlisted men who were housed in the barn. They spread their sleeping bags on the hay and conducted themselves in a proper and orderly fashion. The young soldiers were lots of fun and entertained us with games and laughter. Mostly, they offered us generous amounts of chocolate candy and chewing gum. In fact, after seeing the despair of the German people, U.S. soldiers were supplied with free chocolate and cigarettes and liberally distributed them to the population. Cigarettes soon became a surrogate currency. On the emerging black market goods were paid for in cigarettes. I don't remember any looting or rowdiness as a result of the British occupation in Germany.

Governmental transition came swiftly. All German money was instantly worthless. Each of the ally countries issued their own invasion currency. We were in the British zone, which issued interim legal tender called Reichsmarks. We were required to accept change and adjust without questions. Our life on Rosenhagenstrassee Three did not instantly become beautiful, peaceful, and free. New rules and regulations were put into place. All German borders were closed and the country was sliced into four zones. Russian, British, French, and U.S. zones were quickly established. No one was free to cross from one zone to the next without reams of paperwork and documentation. Families were separated, and jobs were jeopardized. There were many arrests. Monthly passes were necessary to travel between zones and issued only per request by the headquarters of the military government. Each pass was personalized and had to be renewed. The pass permitted the bearer to cross all borders.

After Germany lost the war, the occupying allies divided Germany into four zones and reshaped the borders of Poland.

In a 1 April 1946 letter to the American Property Control Department, Frankfurt/Main, Mother declares the total loss of our home and its worth. The exchange was not one for one, but based on a percentage close to one Reichsmark for four Deutsche Marks. Factories closed, farmers were not producing, and basically, all industry came to a screeching halt. This included coal and peat mining (which we used for heating). As the winter of 1945 approached, the Germans froze and starved, and honest citizens turned to crime for survival. We had less food after the war than during it. In one of Mother's letters, she indicates that she had cultivated a piece of land where she planted potatoes.

5. Nov. '45

I am an American in the employment of the British Military Gov. Hamburg, Esplanade 6, II floor Dept. Public Safety (Special Branch) Tel: 34 10 06—Ext. 260—(Col. Wright). I spent the greater time out in the country during the war, returned to Hamburg in late June of this year. *I planted my own potatoes there and have been permitted to call for at least a part of them.* (Ref: Military Regional Food Office—Mr. Waite) Kindly permit the bearer of this note, Mrs. F. Lemke, with whom I live, to call for same and bring them to me. It is difficult for me to leave my post, and since 4 weeks we have *NOT* one potato in our home. The home (Mrs. Lemke and I) have 6 small children.

Signed
(Mrs.) A. Evans Ritter

Mother, eager to gain employment with the British, gathered her credentials (reissued papers since all our documents were burned) and made haste to get letters of reference into the hands of the British. She applied for a position with Scotland Yard.

We left the Lüneburger Heide and returned to Gross-Flottbek. Keeping all eight of us fed became a constant challenge for Mother and Frau Lemke. With fall coming, the only dependable food supply we had was from Frau Lemke's small home garden, the half-dozen or so fruit trees in the backyard, and whatever we brought back from our occasional trips to Jesteburg. Each year, Frau Lemke hired someone to pick all the fruit and store it in the basement. As we watched the apples and pears ripen, so did someone else. When we got up one morning, we were shocked to see that our fruit trees were almost bare. Someone had come during the night and literally stripped the branches of all fruit. There wasn't much harvest left in the trees or on the ground. However, the thieves left the wooden ladders still propped against the tree trunks. On another occasion, someone in the house noticed an unusually cold draft. After checking the windows, we discovered that someone had broken the glass in the dining-room french doors leading to the back porch. The burglars had entered the house during the night by breaking the glass. All of Frau Lemke's sterling silver, place settings, trays, bowls, crystal, etc., were stolen. We experienced a different type of fear now. I don't even know if Frau Lemke called the police. This was a normal occurrence all over the city. Thieves were hungry neighbors with families to feed. Destitution turned honest families to crime—anything to survive.

Although we had escaped the bombing, new stress and fear came over the population. Foreign military presence was dense. Army jeeps and trucks were full of eager young troops who were jolly and sometimes fresh. Fighting-age adults came under suspicion. The Nazi hunt was on. The National Socialist Party, like the Democratic or Republican parties, was a voluntary organization, but to foreigners, in the aftermath of a hellish war and under intense emotional pressure, all Germans were Nazis.

Georg Mickel-Garbers was the only friend with whom Mother interfaced regularly who was a member of the Nazi Party. Although my father was an officer, he never joined the Nazi Party. His wife, Irmgard von Klitzing, however, was a member of good standing.

The December 2002 edition of the *Smithsonian* has a book excerpt by Michael Beschloss, "Dividing the Spoils," which describes the long and arduous process of reaching a decision regarding Germany's fate after World War II: "In early February of 1945, when the defeat of Germany was finally a foregone conclusion, President Franklin Delano Roosevelt, Prime Minister Winston Churchill and Premier Joseph Stalin met in the Crimean city of Yalta, on the Black Sea, to consider the future of Europe and set the stage for a later meeting at Germany's Potsdam . . . . At Yalta, the leaders of the 'Big

Three' confirmed they would accept nothing less than Germany's unconditional surrender; demand that Germany pay reparations to the victors; and divide the defeated nation into four zones, occupied, respectively, by the United States, Britain, France and the Soviet Union." It took months of difficult and sometimes emotional negotiations. Shortly after the Big Three first met, Franklin D. Roosevelt died and was replaced by Harry S. Truman, and Winston Churchill was voted out of office and replaced by Clement Attlee. Stalin, the most aggressive and vulturous, suggested that Russia take all of the eastern zone and Britain and the United States the western zone. The new leaders agreed. The document was signed on August 1, 1945. The result was that "Stalin took almost one quarter of pre-World War II German territory for Poland. Britain and America, by demanding that each victor seize reparations from its own zone, spared postwar Germany the staggering reparations and debt that, in the 1920s, had brought inflation, unemployment, and Hitler."

It was nearly impossible to cross from one zone to another. The bureaucracy had begun. Basically, we were imprisoned within the British zone, which fortunately incorporated most of our normal traveling territory. On one occasion, however, I remember Mother needed to go to a city within one of the other zones. She had been able to acquire, by special permission, documents to leave the British area and cross the border. She was not able to acquire passes for Klaus and me, but she was eager to take us along. A bread truck driver offered to drive Mother across the border in his truck and said Klaus and I could hide in the back. That was easier said than done. Anyone familiar with the inside of a bread truck knows that the interior is designed with shelves just barely high enough to stack a couple of loaves of bread. On the day of the journey, Mother, with her pass ready, sat in front with the driver. Klaus and I crawled between the shelves and flattened ourselves like ferrets squirming along on our bellies until we were well surrounded on all sides by delicious smelling loaves of bread. The aroma was intoxicating but not quite worth our apprehension that the back of the truck would be searched. Sure enough, as we approached the border, the truck was ordered to stop, and so did our breathing. We heard voices and waited for the sliding side door of the truck to be pulled back at once. I recall seeing a streak of light as a frail attempt was made to slide the door open and peek in, but it seemed more of a routine procedure. Mother and the guard exchanged voices at normal decimal levels. That was always a reassuring sign. Soon the revving gears in the bread truck gave the signal that we were on the move again and could resume breathing.

We had the feeling of living within a military compound. Soldiers and their many vehicles were everywhere checking traffic and enforcing new regulations that appeared stifling and intimidating. Our life changed so drastically. Whereas before we felt alive and unafraid in-between air raids, now we all felt guilty. Personally, their appearance was daunting, but the behavior of the individual soldier was very friendly. I have two letters written in German by Mother requesting the school administration to intervene on her behalf to the overseer of the people's welfare for the purchase of new shoes for Klaus and me. On February 1, 1946, she requests shoes for me, noting that I only had *Gummischuhe* (rubber shoes). On March 6, 1946, she writes that neither Klaus nor I have had a new pair of shoes for two years. The letter explains that we left Hamburg shortly before the war ended and were outside the city; therefore, our *Kleiderkarten* (clothing ration cards) did not permit us to purchase shoes. Also in her files are three United Nations Relief and Rehabilitation Administration permits for supplementary rations. Few items were available without allotment by the British. Food stuffs were rationed according to calories expended by one's profession.

"When NOT using Red Cross parcels, DP [displaced persons] rations will be limited to imported Mil Gov stocks and certain items from German sources in accordance with the following scales."

For a normal consumer, the daily calories were calculated at 1,856. "Moderately heavy workers and camp workers" were allowed 2,379 calories a day. It appears that the largest increase in calories for the "heavy" workers comes from margarine. (The use of the term "pulses" in the chart refers to legumes).

The daily food and energy consumption chart was provided by the British government to assist in the ethical rationing of all food supplies—which were dangerously sparse.

DP/PWX (when in the same Camp)

then NOT using Red Cross parcels, DP rations will be limited to imported Mil Gov stocks and certain items from German sources in accordance with the following scales :

_____

NORMAL CONSUMER

From DIDs:

			Calories
Flour	7 1/2	ozs	728
Preserved Meat	1 1/2	"	105
Pulses	2	"	170
Coffee	1/2	"	-
Sugar	1 1/4	"	135
Tinned Milk	2	"	84
Tinned Fish	5/7	"	34
Jam	1/2	"	35
Salt	3/8	"	-
Margarine	5/7	"	150
Cooking Fat	1/7	"	36
Dehydrated Soup	1	"	120
Dehydrated Egg	3/4	"	111

From German Sources :

Fresh Vegetables	120	grs.	18
Potatoes	200	"	130
			1856

MODERATELY HEAVY WORKER AND CAMP ADM WORKER

From DIDs

Flour	10	ozs	970
Preserved Meat	2	"	140
Pulses	2	"	170
Coffee	1/2	"	-
Sugar	1 1/4	"	135
Tinned Milk	2	"	78
Tinned Fish	5/7	"	34
Jam	1	"	70
Salt	3/8	"	-
Margarine	1 1/2	"	330
Cooking Fat	1/7	"	36
Dehydrated Soup	1	"	120
Dehydrated Egg	1	"	148

From German Sources :

Fresh Vegetables	120	grs	18
Potatoes	200	"	130
			2379

Mother was also eligible for care packages from the Red Cross, which contained mostly food plus some warm clothes and cigarettes. The packages were sent to her office about once a month. The rule in the Lemke house was to share everything. However, often, our cravings for diverse tastes and nutrition overcame our pledge to share. On those occasions, Mother brought the care package to our bedroom, and we ate the contents in secret at night before going to bed. One evening, after the three of us had retired to our room, Mother opened the Red Cross box. Milk was scarce, and we were eager to eat the powdered milk. Although we had a sink in the room, it was still difficult to mix the stuff for drinking. This was before anything instant was invented. The milk was exactly like flour—pasty and lumpy when mixed with water. Consequently, we ate it with a spoon. It was whole milk, rich and delicious. Soon, however, our mouths pasted shut-like with too much peanut butter. Well, wouldn't you know, Frau Lemke knocked on the door. We couldn't even answer her because our jaw teeth and lips were glued shut. Finally, Mother was able to swallow fast and wipe her mouth to answer the door. It was impossible to speak clearly, and Mother knew that we'd been caught. Mother explained that we had gotten hungry and ate her next day's lunch sandwich. Frau Lemke surmised what we did but never spoke of it because she knew she had done exactly the same thing for her children with food that should have been shared equally. Feeding your family at any cost was never considered unscrupulous—even if one had to steal. Forgiveness came quickly among fellow sufferers. The packages from the Red Cross were small, and it took a great deal of discipline to share one chocolate bar or a few crackers with eight people. On the other hand, Mother also received a light woolen set of undergarments. It was a camisole and knee-length drawers. She traded the badly needed set of warm underwear for sugar, which was turned over to Frau Lemke for the good of all.

Border between East and West Germany. The sign reads:
It is also Germany over there;

SCOTLAND YARD

Each new adventure is just one more battle in a long war and it's going to go on as long as we live. "Fight on my men," says Sir Andrew Barton. "I am hurt, but I am not slain; I'll lay me down and bleed awhile, and then rise, and fight again." Quoted in A. E. Ritter's, *Murmurings*, p. 99

THERE WAS SO much turmoil and political confusion immediately following the war that there was no hope for the three of us to return to the United States within the foreseeable future. Mother found permanent employment with the British military government, Administrative Detachment 609, in Hamburg. Her work within the British Intelligence Department required translating correspondence and documents and investigating German political actions to identify Gestapo and Nazi Party members who assisted in war-criminal activities

It appears from the many letters and documents, that Mother spent much of 1945 and 1946 trying to get our citizenship and passport papers in order so we could return to the United States. Also, because the American Consulate closed abruptly, she was owed some severance pay, including vacation time. Mother corresponded with the State Department in America hoping they could help her expedite transportation to the United States and provide her with a job. Another reason our return was delayed, besides the fact that no ships were available for civilians, was Mother's concern for her friends such as Georg Mickel-Garbers, who had by now been arrested. She insisted on being available to testify on his behalf. She attended the trial and bore witness to the fact that Georg Mickel-Garbers had fed and sheltered a family of American citizens during the war and was instrumental in locating Klaus and me after we were kidnapped. As a result of Mother's testimony, Herr Mickel-Garbers was given a reasonably short prison sentence and was released in 1950. Besides Mickel-Garbers, Dr. Matthaei, who represented Mother during the divorce, was also being arrested. The following is an excerpt from a handwritten transcript Mother wrote to the British investigative service in defense of Dr. Matthaei:

> I am an American citizen in the employment of the British Military government, Esplanade 6, II. Special Branch Department, Tel: Ext. 260. This is to testify that Dr. G. Matthaei has been of great assistance to me all during the war as attorney, and as personal advisor—even at his own disadvantage. In June '41 quite alone in Hamburg and without funds, I appealed to Dr. Matthaei, who was a total stranger to me, to represent me in the courts in my efforts to regain possession of my two American-born children who had been stolen from the Diplomatic Train in Frankfurt Main by the Gestapo. This he at once agreed to do without consideration of the consequences which placed him in a politically unsafe position. The opponents as well as the judges in the case were all Party men of high ranks. Dr. Matthaei is generally known in Hamburg as an attorney who acted sympathetically toward Allied and Jewish subjects.

At home, on Rosenhagenstrassee, Klaus and I really were neither aware of what was taking place politically nor of Mother's struggle to regain her footing in the United States. She applied for repatriation with the American Consulate General in Hamburg. She was allotted $500 total: $200 each for her and Klaus, and $100 for me. She had to agree to repay the full sum or never be granted a passport. School was almost nonexistent. Lovesick young British enlisted soldiers frequently hung around the school grounds flirting with the cute girls on the days we assembled. The troops were bored and often truckloads of soldiers cruised the streets. Klaus and I spent more time in Jesteburg, Marxen, and with Oma.

Still nothing from Vati. Oma and Annenie didn't settle into their new location until after we left for the States. They temporarily rented a small stucco cottage in the woods about 50 miles east of Hamburg. My grandmother was raised near Bederkesa and still knew a few familiar names. Their home in Verden was turned over to the railroad workers and quickly converted to a multifamily slum. Finally more than fourteen months after the war ended, our ship was about to come in. It was time to get ready to cross the Atlantic. Mother ordered a deep-freeze sized, custom-made, pig skin shipping trunk. It had thick leather handles on each side and two, wide stainless-steel key locks. This time, culling our possessions was not a difficult task since our inventory had, of course, been involuntarily reduced to mostly our wardrobe. We had accumulated a few personal items besides clothes, such as paintings, photographs, musical instruments, a small lamp, articles we salvaged from the rubble of our home, a clay cake pan, blankets, feather beds, and numerous documents. The trunk and our two cardboard suitcases contained all we had to show for having been more than ten years in Germany—except for our lives, good health, and unforgettable experiences. Mother's well-wishers gave her bon voyage parties. Tante Martha gave her a small framed prayer: *Der Herr ist mein Hirte* (The Lord is my shepherd), and Sepp Ostermayer sketched and printed caricature farewell cards of the three of us waving goodbye as the Statue of Liberty reeled us across the Atlantic.

Departing from Germany, despite the wake of war, was not easy. Many beautiful lifelong relationships had been born during the chaotic times when one seeks condolence, support, shelter, and food from strangers. Bonds are formed under catastrophic conditions that remain unwavering to the end. Emotions ran high, and there were many tears. The chances of Mother ever seeing her companions again were practically nil. Acquaintances appealed to her to relay messages to friends and family in the United States, that they survived. One such request came from a mother who wanted her son, prisoner of war, Käpitanleutenant, Klaus Bargsten, to be notified that she and the family were safe and well.

Friends asked me, "What's the first thing you want when you get to America?" I said, "I want a dog and a black doll." I had only seen dark-skinned people once during our life in Germany. It was at a park, and three or four Africans dressed in conventional wrap were strolling together on the other side of the reflection pool. I thought they were the most interesting and colorful figures I had ever seen. Ever since, I had wanted a black doll that looked like that. Klaus and I positively did not dream or dwell on acquiring material objects or crave special foods. Mostly, we were excited about the trip and eager to embrace anything new.

On June 17, 1946, we sailed to New York from Bremerhaven, Germany, on the troopship, SS *Marine Perch*. The *Marine Perch* was built in 1945 by Kaiser Co., Inc., Richmond, California and was operated in World War II by Grace Line, Inc. She was a C4-S-A3-type ship "Navy allocation." In January 1946 she departed San Francisco for Naples, Italy with a load of Italian prisoners of war. She returned from Naples to New York in February 1946 and was released to the War Shipping Administration which chartered it to United States Lines. The *Marine Perch's* next voyage was from New York City to Bremerhaven where we embarked, and back to New York. The A3s weighed 12,420 gross tons, were 523 feet long, and only 72 feet wide. Maximum passenger capacity was 3,485. After changing ownership several times, the *Marine Perch* was eventually converted to a bulk carrier by Tampa SR & DD Co. in 1965 and renamed *Yellowstone*. In 1978 our refugee ship collided with the ship *Batouta* 14 miles south of Gibraltar and sank the following day whilst in tow.

We had one ticket and one passport for the three of us called a warship ticket from the United States Lines Company. The total cost of the ticket was 500 RM (Reichsmarks); Mother's and Klaus's cost 200 RM each, and my ticket was 100 RM.

Our accommodations aboard ship certainly were not that of a luxury cruise liner. The *Marine Perch* was small compared to most ocean liners today. It was a typical, steel-gray military transport vessel with no frills. We slept on hard, closely quartered bunks and ate in a mess hall with long tables and benches. The tables had rims around all edges so the plates wouldn't slide off. We stood in long mess lines with the other refugees. The weather was reasonably warm on the ocean, but we had a terrible storm during our voyage. Most of the crew and passengers were sick. The morning after the storm the three of us dressed and headed to breakfast, but the mess hall was mostly empty. The minute we smelled the combination of food and vomit, all of us got sick, and we went back to our bunks and stayed there for two days. The fact that our vessel was relatively small exacerbated the sensations of a heaving and falling bow. On calm, sunny days at sea, there barely was standing or sitting room on deck—such as it was. There was little interface with the crew and modest camaraderie among passengers. However, the mood was light. All of the passengers were survivors of some sort and were still basking in their good fortune to be alive and on their way to a new beginning.

I think it took us nearly two weeks to make the voyage. Mother had been corresponding with her brother Fred and sister-in-law Allie Mae Evans in Macon, Georgia, so they would be able to receive and house us until Mother found a job. She had several job interviews pending that friends and former consulate associates had arranged for her. One offer came from the U.S. Veterans Administration in Washington, D.C. In New York, Mother's friend Dr. A. L. Goldwater, MD—Seventy Central Park West, New York, New York—had made arrangements with Lea Goldschmidt for us to stay with her upon our return to the United States. Lea was one of the friends whom Mother helped get out of Germany before most borders were closed.

On June 24, 1946, we received Dr. Goldwater's telegram while onboard the ship, welcoming us to the United States.

Marine Perch

Mother, Klaus and I on deck of the Marine Perch

Lea Goldschmidt

Mackay Radio

SUBSIDIARY OF
AMERICAN CABLE & RADIO CORPORATION
Largest American owned international telegraph system providing worldwide service by cable and radio.

RADIOGRAMS TO ALL PARTS of the WORLD	Commercial Cables	Mackay Radio	SHIP TO SHORE SHORE TO SHIP

All America Cables and Radio

RECEIVED ON BOARD S /S MARINE PERCH   DATE   JJNE 24, 1946

```
AONY DE WIM
PNR7 NEWYORK NY
13 24 847 AM

AURORA RITTER
SS MARINE PERCH
WIM

WELCOME ACCOMMODATIONS READY AT LEA LOVE - DR. GOLDWATER
```

WIM/1540 Z

Mother, Klaus and I on deck of the Marine Perch

STATUE OF LIBERTY

My personal life in a true sense may be divided into
"before" and "after"—Before World War II, and after
the return to the U.S.A. A. E. Ritter, *Murmurings,* p. 167

AS WE APPROACHED New York Harbor, the Statue of Liberty greeted us from Ellis Island on a hot July day in 1946. The skyscrapers, one by one, slowly appeared over the horizon and soon filled the skyline. The SS *Marine Perch* loomed high above the pier as the roaring engines braked the ship. As she cut her speed, she slowly and effortlessly grunted and squeaked into the harbor. It was overwhelming. There were so many new sights and sounds to absorb. We were tense with anticipation. After seeing nothing but water around us for weeks, our cruising into the New York Harbor was awesome. As the *Marine Perch* docked, we looked down from the deck and saw real American people. Except that one time in the park, we had never before seen so many black people. We were spectators looking down on a different world. The men below were working hard, reeling in ropes and pushing dollies and carts loaded with boxes and crates. Most of them wore denim blue shirts and trousers. All the shirts had huge dark blue, almost-black spots on their backs, under the necks, and under the arms. I asked Mother what all those dark spots were. "Das ist Schwitze" (perspiration), she said. Never in my life had I seen sweat like that. In ten years, I never once got warm enough to perspire or saw anyone else with such sweat on their clothes. This was astonishing. Our education was beginning.

After we disembarked, we were met by volunteer workers assigned to aid refugees. They were called the Gray Ladies because they wore gray suits. Mother's pay with the British was issued in Reichmarks and she was told that she could convert the invasion currency to dollars aboard ship or at the port in New York. However, that was not the case and we were literally without a single cent. In order to pay for a taxi to Lea's, Mother had to borrow $1 from one of the Gray Ladies on the dock. It always worried Mother that she did not get the name of the lady and that she was not able to reimburse her the dollar. The cab took us to Lea Goldschmidt's high-rise apartment building at 201 West Eighty-ninth Street, New York, New York. Lea and Mother had a good reunion, but Lea was a spinster who didn't know what to do with children. Her apartment was elegantly furnished. She had a tiny galley kitchen, living room, and two bedrooms. She used one of the bedrooms as her office. Lea was an electrologist. She gave us one bedroom, and she slept in her office. I think we stayed with Lea about a week.

The first day on American soil, Mother left early to tend to some business including the exchange of Reichmarks into dollars. In an 11 July 1946 letter from the law office of O. R. Folsom-Jones, Southern Building, Washington, D.C., it is noted that Mother had received 3,100 Marks in 100 Mark notes issued by the British military in Germany for the exchange into American dollars for not less than $200. In October 1946, O. R. Folsom-Jones returned all of Mother's documentation. I see nothing indicating she ever received the $200. In a May 1948 letter from the Congress of the United States, House of Representatives, a request is made by a friend of Mother's, Mrs. Haviland Haires Lund—337 East Thirty-third Street, New York—on Mother's behalf for back payment by the British government for her intelligence work performed while in Hamburg. In another letter in January 1959, Mother corresponded with the United Kingdom Treasury and Supply Delegation regarding exchanging British military Marks into U.S. dollars. We had no home, money, or job prospects for Mother. Quite simply, we were destitute but not in spirit, health, and enthusiasm. We were survivors. Mother preached that in the big scheme of life, we were rich. Klaus and I had our doubts at times, but we never lacked basic necessities or coveted anything. The word "wish" was not in Mother's vocabulary. She was a doer, not a wisher!

While at Lea's, Klaus and I turned the radio on first thing every morning but couldn't understand a word of English. It seemed like all the Americans were always talking too fast. When we dressed and met Lea, she gave us breakfast. Mother had already left the apartment to tend to more business. Breakfast was Kellogg's cornflakes with milk. This was our first culinary experience in America. Surprised, Klaus and I didn't quite know what to do with these little pieces of crackers floating in cold milk, but we soon understood that you're supposed to eat it that way. When we finished breakfast in Lea's tiny galley kitchen, another new experience for us—eating in a kitchen, we had our first English lesson. Lea said, "Now, children, go outside." Somehow, when you are young and someone speaks a foreign language to you, you know what he or she means even if you don't fully understand each word. Anyway, we understood the message that she didn't want us around, and it was time to make ourselves scarce. Basically, she was sending us out of the apartment into the street, which was okay with us since we were metropolitan kids, concrete kinder, and had been accustomed to large cities, sidewalks, and tall buildings. The multitude of cars, buses, and trucks was stunning and unlike anything we had ever seen due to the lack of benzene in Germany, of course. Without exception, each morning after cornflakes, Miss Goldschmidt said to us, "Now, children, go outside." Naturally, from then on until Lea's death in the early 1970s, Klaus and I only referred to Lea Goldschmidt as "Miss Children Go Outside." Mother explained that the reason Lea wanted us out of the way during the day was because she had customers coming into her apartment and wanted to assure the customers' anonymity. Having unwanted hair removed was a secret, and Miss Children Go Outside was professional. While in New York, Klaus and I quickly became streetwise and scrutinized and explored buildings, shops, and people like two characters in a fast-moving stage scene. It was unbelievably exhilarating and exciting. We saw vending machines for drinks and sandwiches. We saw pinball machines, food at every corner, blinking lights, cars, beggars, people walking fast in all direction, and sounds we had never heard. We were impressed with children playing in the street with powerful bouncing balls. They threw the balls against the houses on the opposite side of the street and caught them as they returned. That first day on the street, Klaus and I needed to know what time it was so we wouldn't get back to Lea's too early or too late. Klaus had had one scant year of English in school, so with his knowledge, we practiced, saying, "Excuse me, what time is it please?" When the test came, we stopped a man in the street and asked him, "What time is it?" We didn't even have to pronounce it twice. We received an immediate reply on our first try, and the man acted as if he didn't even notice that we were "foreigners" or talked peculiar. It worked. We were excited to be communicating in English! Before we left New York on a windy day, the three of us visited the top of the Empire State Building to view the vastness of our new country.

Mother, Klaus and I on the Empire State observation deck, 1946;

EPILOGUE

The only reason I could afford to raise my two children alone, finish my education, and pay off my home, is because I never went to the beauty parlor, never had my nails painted, and never bought an automobile. Aurora Ritter

FROM NEW YORK, we took the train to Washington, D.C., for a short layover where Mother applied for various government positions, but the salary offered to her at the U.S. Veteran's Administration in Washington D. C. was not sufficient to support all three of us, and she declined. We continued our train journey to the Deep South. Atlanta, Georgia, was our next stop. Mother's brother Fred and his youngest son, Maurice, met us in Atlanta and continued the last leg of our journey with us to their home in Macon, Georgia. It was a happy time for Mother, but Klaus and I felt like appendages. We were awkward and frustrated since we could not communicate with our cousin. We took a bus from the Macon train station to my uncle's home where all of the Evans siblings from Georgia and Alabama (five, including Mother) and their families assembled. Although Mother's family was exceptionally kind and loving and tried to give us chocolates and other foods children are supposed to like, the change in culture was overwhelming for us. These people were strangers to Klaus and me. I tended to withdraw and cling to Mother. The heat was unbearable. We enjoyed riding in a car with my cousins and aunt while in Georgia, but I remember being tremendously shy and embarrassed by my inability to converse and avoided eye contact by looking out the window most of the time. My uncle lived in a nice home in a Macon suburb, and Klaus and I soon learned that we were trapped and totally dependent on a grown-up to drive us wherever we wanted to go. The excitement we had become accustomed to during the war years came to an abrupt end and the strain of adjusting to a different culture had its moments of severe stress.

Boletha Frojen, the sister-in-law of Mother's good friend Emily, whom she met in Germany, was able to find an opening for an English teacher at Leon High School in Tallahassee, Florida. Uncle Fred was indebted to Mother for some money he had borrowed during the 1929 Great Depression. With this returned debt, Mother, Klaus, and I settled in Tallahassee. This was not the happiest of times for Klaus and me. It was July or August in Florida. Besides the introduction to hot and humid weather, bedbugs, roaches, fleas, ticks, and other myriads of entomological creatures of gigantic proportions and in mega numbers, there was nothing for us to do. We were restless. In Tallahassee, we had no easy access to bus or train, and of course, Mother could not afford a car. She couldn't even drive. She had not driven since her Model T days in New York. We weren't in a city or on a farm where one has some freedom of movement without a vehicle. The adjustment was rough for all of us. Mother rented a one-room efficiency apartment in a private home for us. We shared our bathroom with the owner's father. But the location was close to the school where Mother would be teaching and about a thirty-minute-walk from our school. It was a primitive and unpleasant setup, but our lifestyle had to match Mother's income. Now in her midforties, she had to start her career all over. Mother took us to Sealy Elementary School to register Klaus and me for the September classes. It was a frightening experience to be exposed to hundreds of scrutinizing eyes.

Not long after Mother began teaching, parents of Mother's pupils complained to the principal because they didn't want a "Nazi" teaching their children. The principal stood by Mother and soon her personality and teaching ability made her one of the more sought after English teachers at Leon High. My salvation during my first year in America was the kindness and acceptance of each student in my fifth-grade class at Sealy School. They were true ambassadors. My fifth-grade teacher, Mrs. Juanita Matthews, was an angel, and my classmates reflected her attitude. I shall remain grateful to all of them. Klaus's situation was more aggressive. He had a difficult teacher, and fell into scraps with other boys but distinguished himself academically and skipped a grade. For Klaus and me, moving from a fast-paced city life to another suburban environment and from a cold climate to tropical Florida was doubly difficult. The regimentation and routine of the same schedule day after day was wearisome yet challenging. Despite the flip-flop of our mental state between thrill and terror during the war, the daily unknown provided us with anticipation and eagerness. We craved adventure. The heat continued to exhaust us, and we had itches and skin rashes we couldn't identify. We had little access to meadows and woods. We tried to take walks in wooded areas but came back with mosquito bites, scratches from underbrush, and embedded ticks.

With roots in Alabama, Mother was in her element. Klaus and I were foreigners. Mother managed her money well, however, and soon we moved into a better home. Also, her long time beau and former fiancé from Montevallo, Alabama reappeared. He was a widower now and ready to renew his relationship with Mother by presenting another offer of marriage. She still had his engagement ring. However, his breath still smelled of alcohol and Mother was not about to compromise her principles for love nor desperately needed money.

Klaus and I had to make significant adjustments. We felt secure being crowded. We liked houses and tall buildings outlined with fences and sidewalks. America was like a fishbowl where things just seem to float together. We missed the structure and security of our confinement in the city. All the foods were more refined and softer and sweeter. We had never heard of biscuits, cornbread, okra, or deep-frying. There were too many choices. Mother was a pioneer in reading labels on all packaged foods and, despite our budget crisis, stressed the importance of not compromising on price where health was concerned. She preached to us to spend more on food and less on doctor bills. Slowly, the good began to outweigh the bad, and we adjusted to our new environment. We were beginning to envision a future. Mother cooked what we were accustomed to such as pan-fried potatoes, red cabbage made with tart apples, black bread, and cheese. For breakfast, we were stuck with cereal. The Americans were very friendly, and nearly all of our contacts were thoughtful and understanding. This genuine kindness had an enormous impact toward our embracing a new and foreign culture. Klaus and I quickly became more proficient in English and were able to meld into the community and participate in social activities.

Each night, Mother, Klaus, and I would sit in bed together and have English lessons. Besides being a busy parent and carrying a full teaching schedule, Mother went back to college and completed the needed credits for her bachelor's degree in English and continued to complete her master's degree in psychology from Florida State University (FSU) in 1952. Mother literally worked day and night: teaching school all day, grading English papers, attending classes at night, preparing our meals, and helping us with lessons. After a busy day at work, she walked several miles from Leon High School to attend evening classes at FSU and then walked home again late evenings after class. Sometimes she would get a ride, but often, Mother didn't get home until nearly midnight. She wrote her dissertation at night, frequently setting up a small table in the bathroom so the clacking of her old Underwood typewriter wouldn't disturb our sleep. She would never have dreamed of asking for or accepting any type of financial assistance. She was much too proud. In summers, Mother taught a few English and geography classes, worked for the State of Florida, and was a camp counselor for Leon County, Florida. Until her retirement, in 1970, Mother's vacations were limited to family visits in Georgia and Alabama. She found no time for self pity.

After we settled into our second home in Tallahassee, on Cherry Street, another suitor entered Mother's life. One of our neighbors, a bachelor banker living with his spinster sister, proposed marriage to Mother. Unfortunately, she discussed his proposition with Klaus and me and the three of us decided that as kind as he was, he didn't fit into our history and therefore not into our future. Klaus and I have always regretted this decision—even at her funeral. He was a wonderful person and would have provided devoted companionship for our Mother. I believe that Mother's total focus was always her children and therefore she could not defend any act that might give her the sensation of self serving.

Klaus and I also worked outside of school. Some of the local churches gave us clothes. We held odd jobs until we were old enough to be legally employed after school and during summers. Klaus had paper routes, worked for a Studebaker dealership, assembled and repaired pinball machines for Fred Deeb Amusement Company, and bought the only car we ever owned. I worked in a bank and for the State of Florida during summers, and wrapped gift packages for a department store on holiday breaks. On Saturdays, Mother washed our clothes in the bathtub with a plunger, hung them out to dry, and I did the family ironing.

Eventually, my wish came true, and we got our first dog named Jigs. He was a tiny black-and-white waggish looking puppy with a dull facial expression. That school year, the only day Mother stayed home from her job was when Jigs had distemper. Mother was a great believer in Vicks salve. She rubbed his neck and nose with Vicks salve and wrapped a wool (it had to be wool) scarf around his neck and held him on her lap for nearly twenty four hours. Jigs smelled like an apothecary for days, but he survived. Also, Aunt Annie, Mother's sister from Alabama, was able to find a Negro doll for me. Emma is about fifteen inches tall. She is clad in a light blue-and-white polka-dot organdy dress, matching hat, and white shoes. Except for a few hairline cracks across her face, she hasn't aged much. Emma now sits in a prominent location in my daughter's home. In 1958, Mother bought her own home and paid the mortgage off in record time. She repeatedly exclaimed that the reason she never "owed a penny" in her life was because she never bought a car (postwar) and never went to the hairdressers.

My husband, our two children, and I made several visits to Germany before my grandmother died in the summer of 1969 at age ninety-four. Annenie and Hans (who now went by the name of Fritz, mysteriously reappeared) lived together in Uelzen, Germany, until their deaths in the mid 1990s. Klaus and I, and my two children have continued contact with our German cousins and their children. Georg Mickel-Garbers wrote Mother when he was released from prison. He and his wife are both deceased now. Mother carried on correspondence with his daughters. After a prolonged illness, Tante Martha Unteutsch passed away in the mid 1970s. Onkel Erhard Unteutsch received a speeding ticket on his way to work at the tea factory when he was ninety-nine. He died at age one hundred. He and Mother wrote regularly to each other until his death. When my son visited the Unteutsch family in 1994, Erhard eagerly engaged him by reminiscing and showing him all the family pictures, including those of Mother, Klaus, and me. Erica Mickel-Garbers Artman, Georg's daughter, was equally gracious to my son on his visit to Germany. Karen, our half sister, also hosted my son for several days. As we became more involved in our American life, we lost much of our ability to speak and write in German. Even Mother had difficulty writing freely in German, and this made it awkward to maintain a vigorous correspondence with the past.

After Vati's plane crash in the desert, he could not continue undercover work and was made commander in a Luftwaffe Panzer Division and took part in the battle of Sicily. Near the end of the war, he was a *Brigadeführer* (brigade commander) with two flak regiments containing Panzer and Luftwaffe groups. They were surrounded and taken prisoner by American troops in the Harz Mountains on April 20, 1945. On May 9, 1945, Mother received a letter from Vati, saying he had not been able to send her any money since he had been ill. He wrote that when he finally went to the bank to withdraw some money his account was blocked, but he would send her some money when he found a job with the military government. Vati, recognized for his excellent command of American English, was employed by the U.S. Army as a translator until he was arrested by British troops and placed in Neuengamme Prison Camp, which was converted into a prisoner-of-war camp. Klaus and I were told nothing of this and for some reason were kept in the dark about Vati's existence. Apparently after Mother discovered that Vati was arrested and in prison, she concurred with Oma that we children should not be told. If asked, it was safer to say our father was lost in the war than to say he was in prison. Neuengamme was used during the war to house mostly criminals and political prisoners. War-time inmates at Neuengamme were used primarily for labor and to clean cities of debris and carnage left from air raids. After Vati was released on May 22, 1947, Oma sent us a letter letting us know that Vati was well and that he and Irmgard were living in Gross-Flottbek. Both Vati and Hans received pensions from the German government. Also, Annenie received a pension for caring for her mother, which was considered legitimate employment. In his postwar career, Vati worked for a charitable organization, Hilfsgemeinschaft (help or aid organization), in Hamburg. He was responsible for financial distributions made to third-world countries. In 1959, we saw Vati for the first time in more than fifteen years. He arrived on a Likes Shipping Line carrier at the Humble Oil Refinery Company docks in Baton Rouge, Louisiana. Klaus, my husband, and I drove from Tallahassee to Baton Rouge to meet him. Our time was limited, and the meeting was somewhat estranged but friendly. An FBI agent approached us as we walked from the docks to a nearby cafeteria. He said, "Hello, Mr. Ritter, how long are you planning to be in the country?" Vati had a valid German passport and assured the agent that it would only be a couple of days. We grew closer over time and continued our relationship by mail and infrequent visits. Irmgard was always pleasant and correct to us. While in one of the third-world countries, Vati contracted a virus and died unexpectedly on 25 March 1974. We remained friendly with Irmgard until her death in spring of 1997.

Klaus graduated from Georgia Tech, met a German girl at FSU, and moved back to Germany. He received an architectural engineering degree from the Art Academy of Berlin and has a private practice in Berlin. Currently, he and his wife have homes in Berlin, Germany, and in Cortona, Italy. I received my undergraduate in arts and education from FSU and received a master of science degree From Louisiana State University in library science. I studied one year in Kentucky, where I met my husband. We now live in McLean, Virginia. Our son and his family live in Springfield, Virginia, and our daughter and her husband reside in Alexandria, Virginia. Mother's home was directly across from Carolyn Brevard School in Tallahassee where she taught until her retirement on June 10, 1970. She lived a full active life and enjoyed many friends; her yard; books; and, most of all, her family. These were her therapy and mentors. She kept abreast of all political events and wrote frequent letters to her congressional representatives. At age eighty, she decided to move back to Barbour County, Alabama. She made her new and final home in Wesley Manor, Dothan, Alabama. In 1980, Mother—accompanied by my husband, our two children, and me—returned to Germany for the first time since she left in 1946. For her ninetieth birthday, I took Mother to Italy to celebrate with Klaus and his wife in their hilltop home in Tuscany. Preceded by all her siblings, our mother passed away peacefully on January 11, 1997, at age ninety-eight.

Vati and I with my husband (right), 1959

Mother was a prodigious writer. She credits her one-room schoolhouse with her ability to memorize. After some persuasion from her family, at age ninety-four, Mother compiled handwritten manuscripts, from memory, of all poems memorized by her, including prayers in German and English and those she wrote herself. The index lists 109. At her ninetieth birthday party, she stood in front of her family and recited all nine verses of Henry W. Longfellow's (1807-1881) "A Psalm of Life." She wanted "Crossing the Bar" by Alfred Lord Tennyson and the closing lines of "Thanatopsis" by William Cullen Bryant read at her funeral:

So live that when the summons comes to join
The innumerable caravan that moves
To that mysterious realm, where each shall take
His chamber in the silent halls of death,
Thou go not like the quarry-slave at night,
Scourged to his dungeon, but, sustained and soothed
By an unfaltering trust, approach thy grave
Like one who wraps the drapery of his couch
About him, and lies down to pleasant dreams.

All of Mother's family, friends, and acquaintances fortunate enough to have received correspondence from her told me they have saved all she ever wrote to them. Klaus and his wife have compiled a booklet entitled *Letters Sage from a Mother*. When she was ninety-five years of age, she wrote to Klaus:

I have very good days and some not so good, only trivial discomforts. But I still love LIFE and find my precious loved ones to be God's Chosen People. I'm at peace when my children are well and healthy.

In another publication, *Brief Heritage Résumé for My Two Beloved Grandchildren*, Mother writes about her family:

Ours is an unusual family—remarkably stable, durable, healthy, and strong—no closet skeletons. I feel that our fore-parents would be duly pleased. My cup runneth o'er!

In *A Brief Resume of a Life Worth the Living*, Mother writes:

I think there's a need deep down inside of everyone to say, I'm proud of who I am and from whence I came. Now in the closing years of my life, I salute with increasing appreciation the village community life of my youth and that of my fore parents.

Mother was true to herself. She lived by her own convictions of worthiness. Her character was solid and honorable. She was confident and proud of doing what was right to the best of her knowledge. The week before her death, Mother and I sat alone on the terrace of her retirement home and silently watched the evening sun fade behind the horizon. Her clear blue eyes lingered intently on the sharp January sky all washed with wild streaks of white and pink, when she reminisced slowly and with deliberation, "I think I would do everything in my life the same all over again." "Yes" she continued thoughtfully, "I think I would."

Mother was always drawn to her home in the Deep South and frequently expressed being fortified by the presence of her mother's spirit. Despite the extreme emotional pain, she considered her life's journey around the globe and back to Barbour County a success and never failed to be grateful for the least little favor. In "A Letter to Her Children," Mother says, "If one may evaluate his virtues, I'd like to claim for myself (1) courage (2) humility (3) compassion for all mankind, and (4) gratitude."

Having come full circle by detour of World War II, she wanted to return to the source of her strength and faith and let her spirit wander among the trees where she learned to love life. She lies buried in the Perkins-Evans Cemetery, which was once called Zion's Chapel, in White Oak Springs, Barbour County, Alabama, a few yards from where she was born and close to the large magnolia tree under which she played as a child.

She believed passionately the words she had engraved on her tombstone:

> The sprit of my forefathers,
> My family, my friends, and my
> Beloved children will be
> My comrades and speak to me
> In the silence of the nights.

Aurora, 1918

SOURCES

Beschloss, Michael. "Dividing the Spoils." Book excerpt, *The Smithsonian*. Dec. 2002. p. 111.

Charles, Roland W. *Troopships of World War II*. Washington, DC: The Army Transportation Association, Washington, DC, 1947. p. 213.

Carell, Paul. *The Foxes of the Desert*. New York: Bantam Books, Inc., 1960. p. 369.

Elsevier International Projects, Ltd. *Harver World Encyclopedia*. New York: Harver Educational Services, Inc., 1976. pp. 4,076-4,079.

Farago, Ladislas. *The Game of the Foxes*. New York: Bantam Books, Inc., 1971. p. 878.

Ritter, Aurora Evans. *A Brief Heritage Resumé for My Two Beloved Grandchildren, Raymond H. Wallace III and Mary Haviland Wallace*. (Unpublished)

Ritter, Klaus H. *Letters Sage from a Mother*. (Unpublished)

Ritter, Nikolaus. *Deckname Dr. Rantzau*. Hamburg: Hoffmann und Campe Verlag, 1972. p. 327.

Ronnie, Art. *Counterfeit Hero: Fritz Duquesne, Adventurer and Spy*. Annapolis: Naval Institute Press, 1995. p. 390.

Sawyer, L. A. and Mitchell, W. H. *From America to United States.* Kendal, England: World Ship Society, 1981. p. 74

Seabald, W. G. "A Natural History of Destruction." *The New Yorker.* Nov 4, 2002. p. 66.

Thomson, Alfred Ray. *Historical Letters.* Compiled by Mrs. A. R. Thomson. New York: Hobson Book Press, 1946. p. 178.

Whiting, Charles. *Canaris.* New York: Ballantine Books, Inc., 1973. p. 264.

Wells, Joanne L. "Tales of Horror, Wonder Recounted." *The Dothan Eagle.* July 1, 1991.

U.S. National Archives and Records Administration. Records of the Defense Intelligence Agency College Park, Maryland. March 1945. Record Group 373.

Valour and the Horror (The). A Mental Blocks Production. *Bomber Command.* GoodRobot Community Learning Network. Canada: St. Christopher House. 2004. www.valourandhorror.com

Other sources:
    Letters from Mother to her family and friends, and copies of business letters.
    Aurora's obituary
    Notes from interviews with Mother and other relatives.

Cover: Design by the author
    Background image: *Hamburg, Germany 1945.* Courtesy of the U.S. Naval Historical Center Photography Section, Washington, D.C.
    Foreground images: Aurora Evans Ritter and Nikolaus A. F. Ritter.

BVG